NEW
CHILDREN'S
PARTY CAKES

NEW CHILDREN'S PARTY CAKES

35 STEP-BY-STEP RECIPES

Joanna Farrow

EBURY PRESS
LONDON

First published in 1998

1 3 5 7 9 10 8 6 4 2

First published in the United Kingdom in 1998 by Ebury Press
Random House, 20 Vauxhall Bridge Road, London SW1V 2SA

Random House Australia (Pty) Limited
20 Alfred Street, Milsons Point, Sydney,
New South Wales 2061, Australia

Random House New Zealand Limited
18 Poland Road, Glenfield,
Auckland 10, New Zealand

Random House South Africa (Pty) Limited
Endulini, 5a Jubilee Road,
Parktown 2193, South Africa

Random House UK Limited Reg. No. 954009

A CIP catalogue record for this book is available from the British Library.

ISBN 0 09 186498 4

Edited by Rosie Hankin
Designed by Jerry Goldie Graphic Design
Photography by Tom Gordon
Techniques photography by Karl Adamsom

Printed and bound in Singapore by Tien Wah Press

The following cakes were devised and supplied by Polly Tyrer:
Kitten Castle, page 28; Toadstool, page 34; Robot, page 42; Animal Carousel, page 50; Friendly Tiger, page 58; Haunted Castle, page 64; Muncher, page 74; Dinosaur Egg, page 80; Wrestling Ring, page 88.

CONTENTS

INTRODUCTION

Novelty cakes are usually the main focus of a child's birthday celebration and will often produce squeals of delight, especially if the cake is specially designed for the recipient. Making a children's party cake yourself is very rewarding and can be enormous fun, whether you are experienced cake decorator or a complete novice. Never be put off by lack of expertise; practice makes perfect and even if you don't achieve perfection first time round, a home-made, personalized cake will always be a success. This book contains a wide selection of imaginative ideas; for very young children there are simple, boldly coloured cakes such as First Telephone or fun-shaped Happy House, while for older children there are plenty of exciting ideas such as Keyboard, Football Mad or the beautifully wrapped Birthday Present. All the cakes have been designed with speed and simplicity in mind. They're made using basic sponge cake recipes which are provided, and are then assembled following simple step-by-step techniques. If the chosen cake is round or square you can easily take shortcuts by using a bought sponge or fruit cake.

Before you start, check the recipe for any special instructions like letting icing decorations harden overnight, or using special ingredients such as an unusual food colouring. All the ingredients and pieces of equipment used are widely available in supermarkets and cake decorating shops, but a mail order supply list is included at the back of the book for convenience. Most of the cakes are decorated with ready-to-roll icing, one of the easiest and most effective icings available. Rolled out and draped over a cake it provides a smooth covering as well as being excellent for moulding stunning figures and decorations. As you will soon discover, its simplicity and effectiveness bring out a creativity in even the least experienced cake decorator.

Whatever your level of skill, there is something here to delight every child and give you pleasure in the making.

Joanna Farrow

EQUIPMENT

Very little specialist equipment is needed to make the cakes in this book, but if you intend to make cakes regularly it is well worth building up a collection of useful gadgets, both to make decorating easier and to give better results.

1 Tins and moulds

Most of the cakes are baked in square, round or sandwich tins. Buy good quality, sturdy tins which retain their shape however much they are used and that won't rust during storage. A few of the cakes are baked in Pyrex ovenproof mixing bowls or pudding bowls. Don't use a bowl unless you are sure it is ovenproof.

2 Turntable

A cake turntable makes decorating much easier as the cake can be rotated effortlessly, without any risk of damaging the icing at the edges of the board.

3 Cake boards

Boards are available in all shapes and sizes, either as thin cards or thicker drums. For most cakes the board is usually 5 cm (2 inches) bigger than the cake itself. For presentation, cover the edges of the board with a thin layer of icing and place a ribbon around the sides, securing at the back with double-sided tape or dressmakers' pins.

4 Grater

5 Tins (see above)

6 Hand mixer

This takes the hard work out of creaming together butter and sugar, whisking eggs or making butter cream or royal icing. Always use softened butter or margarine to get a really light, creamy result.

7 Measuring jug

8 Brown paper

9 Measuring spoons

These are essential for measuring accurately small quantities of ingredients, such as vanilla and almond essence, baking powder and lemon juice.

10 Cutters

These are available in many shapes and sizes and are really useful for quick and easy novelty cakes. A set of plain round cutters makes light work of shaping clean-cut circles of icing.

11 Knives

A large knife, plain edged or serrated, is good for cutting sponges into novelty shapes, or slicing for sandwiching with fillings. A small, fine bladed knife or scalpel is essential for cutting out small, decorative pieces of icing.

12 Ruler and pencil

A ruler is necessary for measuring decorative icing shapes and tin sizes. You will need a pencil for drawing around tins when lining with greaseproof paper and designing templates.

13-14 Palette knives

Available in small, medium and large sizes, palette knives are useful for spreading jam , butter cream and royal icing, and for loosening cakes from tins. A

cranked handle palette knife is useful for spreading icing and smoothing it out without your hands touching the surface of the icing.

15 Spatulas

Made with a very flexible, plastic blade, spatulas are useful for scraping cake mixtures and icing from a bowl so that none of the mixture is wasted.

16 Wooden spoons

Keep a selection of various sized spoons for mixing different quantities of cake mixtures and sponges.

17 Scissors

You will need scissors for cutting out greaseproof paper piping bags, templates and paper for tin lining.

18 Nylon piping bags

For piping cream, butter cream and royal icing, nylon bags are useful as they can be washed and reused. For small quantities of royal icing and butter cream, a greaseproof paper piping bag is easy to make and use (see box, right).

19 Metal piping nozzles

These are available in many shapes and sizes for piping cream, butter cream and royal icing. A medium (no. 2) plain writing nozzle is the easiest to use for piping messages and simple details on to novelty cakes.

20 Bowls

Keep a selection of different sized bowls for mixing cakes and icings.

21 Sieve

A sieve is needed for sifting flour into cake mixes. Icing sugar needs sifting as it tends to settle into lumps during storage.

22 Wrapping

Cling film is essential for wrapping ready-to-roll icing tightly while it is not in use, as it quickly forms a dry crust if left unwrapped. Foil is good for wrapping cakes until you are ready to decorate them. Greaseproof paper is used for lining cake tins and making piping bags. Non-stick baking parchment has a non-stick coating, ideal for resting icing decorations on until you are ready to transfer them to the cake.

23 Wire racks

Most sponge cakes are removed from their tins as soon as they are baked (to prevent further cooking in the hot tin) and transferred to a wire rack so the air can circulate and cool the cake quickly.

24 Glazing brushes

Buy good quality brushes which are less likely to shed their bristles during use. Use for brushing tins with

TO MAKE A GREASEPROOF PAPER PIPING BAG

1 Cut a 23 cm (9 inch) square of greaseproof paper, then cut the square in half diagonally to make two triangles.

2 Hold one triangle with the long side away from you and fold the left-hand point over to meet the bottom point, curling the paper round to make a cone shape.

3 Fold the right-hand point over the cone, bringing all three points together. Fold the points over several times to secure the bag.

4 Cut off 1 cm ($\frac{1}{2}$ inch) from the tip of the bag and fit with a piping nozzle. Alternatively, fill with butter cream or icing and cut off the merest tip so the icing can be piped in a thin line.

melted fat when lining them and for brushing cakes with jam, honey or glaze.

25 Thermometer

26 Whisks

A large whisk is useful for beating a cake mixture to achieve a smooth result if you don't have an electric whisk. Smaller whisks are good for beating butter cream and icings.

BASIC TECHNIQUES

Mastering a few simple techniques will make the difference between failures and suuccessful cakes.

LINING BAKING TINS

Baking tins and other containers must be prepared correctly for successful results. Follow the simple procedures set out below and your cakes should rise beautifully during baking.

DEEP CAKE TINS

Place the tin on a piece of greaseproof paper and draw around it. Cut out the shape just inside the marked line. Cut a strip of paper long enough to line the sides of the tin and about 2.5 cm (1 inch) deeper. Make a 2.5 cm (1 inch) fold along one long edge of the strip and snip the folded portion from the edge to the fold at 2.5 cm (1 inch) intervals. Grease the base and sides of the tin with melted fat or oil and fit the strip of paper around the sides so the fold sits in the bottom of the tin and the snipped edges rest on the base. Press the cut-out round or square of greaseproof paper into the base of the tin. Brush the paper with more fat or oil.

NOTE: Greasing the lining paper is essential, particularly with sponge cakes as they will not rise properly if baked in a non-greased tin.

SANDWICH TINS

Only line the base of the tins with greaseproof paper, then brush both the paper and sides of the tin with melted fat or oil.

TIPS FOR PREPARING THE CAKES

● Make sure the tin is properly lined and the paper is greased, otherwise the cake will not rise properly during baking.
● Check the cake shortly before the end of the recommended baking time as ovens do vary. To test whether a Victoria sandwich cake - the traditional or quick-mix method – is done, press very gently on the centre of the cake with your fingers. The sponge should spring back. For a Madeira cake, the surface of the cake should be a deep golden colour and should feel firm to the touch.
● Most cakes are best transferred to a wire rack to cool. Loosen the edges of the cake and carefully invert the cake on to the rack. For cakes baked in ovenproof bowls, leave them to cool in the bowl, otherwise they might loose their rounded shape.
● Cakes that are to be cut into novelty shapes are best baked a day in advance as they will have firmed up slightly and will be easier to cut.
● The tops of Madeira cakes often dome slightly during baking. Once cooled, slice off the risen dome before continuing with the recipe.
● All the sponges can be stored, well wrapped in their lining paper and kitchen foil, for up to a week before decorating. Freeze the cake if you intend storing it for longer.

SHALLOW RECTANGULAR TINS

Grease the tin and press a rectangle of greaseproof paper, measuring 7.5 cm (3 inches) longer and wider than the tin. Press the paper into the corners, snipping to fit. Grease the paper.

LOAF TINS

Grease the tin and line with a strip of greaseproof paper which covers the base of the tin and the long sides. Grease the paper.

OVENPROOF BOWLS

Grease the bowl and cut out a circle of greaseproof paper which covers the base and slightly up the sides. Make 2.5 cm (1 inch) cuts from the edge of the circle towards the centre at 2.5 cm (1 inch) intervals. Fit into the base and grease the paper.

USING FOOD COLOURINGS

There are several different types of food colourings available in supermarkets and cake decorating shops.

LIQUID COLOURINGS

These are the type of colourings that supermarkets stock. Very thin in strength, a few drops can be used to colour glacé or royal icing to a pastel shade. You won't achieve rich, vibrant colours, however much you use.

CONCENTRATED LIQUID COLOURINGS

These are usually only available in cake decorating shops and come in a wide range of colours. They can be used to colour butter cream, glacé icing, royal icing and ready-to-roll icing. Use a cocktail stick to dot ready-to-roll icing with colouring, then knead in on a surface dusted with icing sugar until the icing is no longer streaked with colour.

PASTE COLOURINGS

These are a very concentrated range of colourings that come in a smooth, gel-like paste. They can be used to colour all types of icing, whether you want a very delicate shade, or a rich, bold one. Use very cautiously at first until you are sure of the strength of the paste. Apply as for concentrated liquid colourings.

DUSTING POWDERS

These are edible, coloured powders which can either be kneaded into ready-to-roll icing or brushed on to finished decorations. There are several different types available; some give a matt finish, while others give a pearlised, metallic or sparkle finish. Gold and silver dusting powder is particularly effective. To use, mix a little dusting powder with a few drops of groundnut or sunflower oil, or a clear alcohol, to give a thin paste-like consistency. Apply with a fine brush.

FOOD COLOURING PENS

These are used like ordinary fibre tip pens and are available in most popular colours. Use to write messages and names or to draw patterns directly on to set royal or ready-to-roll icing.

MIXING FOOD COLOURINGS

You can still achieve a good variety of different colours even with just a few basic liquid or paste colours. Remember that you can mix blue and yellow to make green, red and yellow to make orange, green and yellow to make lime green, and blue and green to make sea green. Some of the recipes use light and dark shades of a particular colour. Simply work in more colouring to achieve a darker shade. When colouring icing, bear in mind that most colours will darken slightly as they dry out.

TIPS FOR USING READY-TO-ROLL ICING

- Cake decorating shops sell a wide range of coloured ready-to-roll icing, which saves a lot of kneading time. The smallest packet sizes are usually 225 g (8 oz). Supermarkets also sell mixed packets of ready-coloured icings, but in a limited range of colours.
- When not in use the icing should be wrapped immediately in cling film as it quickly develops a hard crust if left exposed. Once wrapped it can be stored in a cool place for several weeks.
- Both icing sugar and cornflour can be used when rolling the icing. Icing sugar should be used when applying a layer of icing to the cake. Cornflour gives better results for smoothing the icing and shaping decorations.
- Partially kneading food colouring into ready-to-roll icing gives an interesting streaked result which can look effective on novelty cakes when you want to depict such things as wood or water.
- Use fine bladed, sharp knives to give a good, clean edge when cutting and shaping the icing. A blunt or round ended knife might tear the icing and will not enable you to get into corners.

COVERING A CAKE
WITH READY-TO-ROLL
ICING

With a little practice it is not difficult to achieve a really smooth finish on ready-to-roll icing. The secret is to avoid rolling the icing too thinly which makes all the lumps and bumps on the cake show through. Spend a little time smoothing the icing with the palms of your hands as their warmth gradually eliminates any creases or wrinkles in the icing. Finally, an icing smoother, a flat plastic tool with a handle, can be worked over the icing to give a really professional-looking finish.

1 Place the cake on the board and spread with honey, apricot glaze or butter cream. Knead the ready-to-roll icing lightly into a smooth ball.

2 Roll out the ready-to-roll icing on a surface dusted with icing sugar to a round or square about 7.5 cm (3 inches) larger than the diameter of the cake. Roll the icing loosely around the rolling pin and lift it over the top of the cake. Carefully unroll the icing so it falls evenly around the sides of the cake.

3 Using hands dusted with cornflour smooth the icing over the top of the cake and around the sides, easing it to fit and, where necessary, smoothing away any creases. Trim off any excess icing around the base of the cake. Using lightly cornfloured hands or a cake smoother, gently smooth the surface of the icing in a circular movement until completely smooth.

BASIC RECIPES

All the party cakes in this book use one of the basic cake recipes that follow. The fillings and icings are also given.

VICTORIA SANDWICH CAKE

This popular English cake may be made by the traditional or quick-mix method. Both produce a light sponge which may be flavoured and cooked in different shapes and sizes of tins

TRADITIONAL METHOD

175 g (6 oz) butter or block margarine, softened

175 g (6 oz) caster sugar

3 eggs, beaten

175 g (6 oz) self-raising flour, sifted

1 Grease and base line two 18 cm (7 inch) sandwich tins with greaseproof paper or non-stick baking parchment. Grease the paper.

2 Beat the butter or margarine and sugar together until pale and fluffy. Add the eggs, a little at a time, beating well.

3 Fold in half the flour, using a spatula, then fold in the remainder it is incorporated.

4 Divide the mixture evenly between the tins and level with a palette knife. Bake in the centre of the oven at 180°C (350°F) Mark 4 for 25-30 minutes until the cakes are well risen and spring back when lightly pressed in the centre. Loosen the edges of the cakes with a palette knife and leave in the tins for 5 minutes. Turn out, invert on to a wire rack, remove the lining paper and leave to cool.

VARIATIONS
Chocolate – Replace 45 ml (3 tbsp) flour with sifted cocoa powder.
Coffee – Blend together 10 ml (2 tsp) instant coffee

granules with 15 ml (1 tbsp) boiling water. Cool and add to the creamed mixture with the eggs.
Citrus – Add the finely grated rind of an orange, lime or lemon to the mixture.

QUICK-MIX METHOD

175 g (6 oz) self-raising flour

5 ml (1 tsp) baking powder

175 g (6 oz) caster sugar

175 g (6 oz) soft margarine

3 eggs, beaten

1 Grease and base line two 18 cm (7 inch) sandwich tins with greaseproof paper or non-stick baking parchment. Grease the paper

2 Sift the flour and baking powder into a bowl. Add the sugar, margarine and eggs. Mix with a wooden spoon, beat for 1-2 minutes until smooth and glossy, or use an electric mixer or food processor.

3 Bake as for the traditional method (see step 4).

MADEIRA CAKE

This is a good moist plain cake which has a firm texture, making it a good base for a celebration cake. There are many variations for flavouring. Use the traditional or quick-mix method and flavour if you wish. Refer to the cake chart opposite for sizes and quantities

TRADITIONAL METHOD
1 Grease and line a deep cake tin following the instructions on page 11.

2 Sift the flours together. Cream the butter and

sugar in a bowl until pale and fluffy. Add the eggs, a little at a time, beating well after each addition.

3 Fold in the flour with a plastic spatula, adding a little lemon juice or milk if necessary to give a dropping consistency. Add any flavourings if required.

4 Turn the mixture into the prepared tin and spread evenly. Give the tin a sharp tap to remove any air pockets. Make a depression in the centre of the mixture to ensure a level surface.

5 Bake in the centre of the oven at 170°C (325°F) Mark 3 following the chart baking times, or until the cake springs back when lightly pressed in the centre.

6 Leave the cake to cool in the tin, then remove and cool completely on a wire rack. Wrap in cling film or foil and store in a cool place until required.

VARIATIONS

These flavourings are for a 3-egg quantity of Madeira cake. Increase the suggested flavourings to suit the quantities being made.

Cherry – add 175 g (6 oz) glacé cherries, halved.

Coconut – add 50 g (2 oz) desiccated coconut.
Nut – replace 125 g (4 oz) flour with ground almonds, hazelnuts, walnuts or pecan nuts.
Citrus – add the grated rind and juice of 1 lemon, orange or lime.

QUICK-MIX METHOD

1 Grease and line a deep cake tin following the instructions on page 11.

2 Sift the flours into a mixing bowl, add the butter or margarine, sugar, eggs and lemon juice or milk. Mix with a wooden spoon, then beat for 1-2 minutes until smooth and glossy. Alternatively, use an electric mixer and beat for 1 minute only. Add any flavourings if required and mix until well blended.

3 Turn the mixture into the prepared tin and spread evenly. Give the tin a sharp tap to remove any air pockets. Make a depression in the centre of the mixture to ensure a level surface.

4 Bake as for the traditional method (see steps 5 and 6).

MADEIRA CAKE CHART

CAKE TIN SIZE	15 cm (6 in) square 18 cm (7 in) round	18 cm (7 in) square 20.5 cm (8 in) round	20.5 cm (8 in) square 23 cm (9 in) round	23 cm (9 in) square 25.5 cm (10 in) round
Plain flour	125 g (4 oz)	175 g (6 oz)	225 g (8 oz)	250 g (9 oz)
Self-raising flour	125 g (4 oz)	175 g (6 oz)	225 g (8 oz)	250 g (9 oz)
Unsalted butter, softened, or soft margarine	175 g (6 oz)	275 g (10 oz)	400 g (14 oz)	450 g (1 lb)
Caster sugar	175 g (6 oz)	275 g (10 oz)	400 g (14 oz)	450 g (1 lb)
Eggs, size 3	3	5	7	8
Lemon juice or milk	30 ml (2 tbsp)	45 ml (3 tbsp)	52.5 ml (3½ tbsp)	60 ml (4 tbsp)
Baking time (approx.)	1¼ – 1½ hours	1½ – 1¾ hours	1¾ – 2 hours	1¾ – 2 hours

CAKE TIN SIZE	25.5 cm (10 in) square 28 cm (11 in) round	28 cm (11 in) square 30.5 cm (12 in) round	30.5 (12 in) square 33 cm (13 in) round
Plain flour	275 g (10 oz)	350 g (12 oz)	450 g (1 lb)
Self-raising flour	275 g (10 oz)	350 g (12 oz)	450 g (1 lb)
Unsalted butter, softened, or soft margarine	500 g (1 lb 2 oz)	625 g (1 lb 6 oz)	725 g (1 lb 10 oz)
Caster sugar	500 g (1 lb 2 oz)	625 g (1 lb 6 oz)	725 g (1 lb 10 oz)
Eggs, size 3	10	12	13
Lemon juice or milk	67.5 ml (4½ tbsp)	75 ml (5 tbsp)	82.5 ml (5½ tbsp)
Baking time (approx.)	2-2¼ hours	2¼ - 2½ hours	2½ - 2¾ hours

APRICOT GLAZE

It is always a good idea to make a large quantity of apricot glaze, especially when making a celebration cake.

450 g (1 lb) apricot jam
30 ml (2 tbsp) water

1 Place the jam and water into a saucepan and heat gently, stirring occasionally, until melted.

2 Boil the jam rapidly for 1 minute, then strain through a sieve. Rub through as much fruit as possible, using a wooden spoon. Discard the skins left in the sieve.

3 Pour the glaze into a clean, hot jar, then seal with a clean lid and cool. It will keep in the fridge for up to 2 months.

4 Use to brush cakes before applying marzipan, and for glazing fruit finishes on gâteaux and cakes.
Makes 450 g (1 lb) apricot glaze

ROYAL ICING
(FRESH EGG WHITES)

2 size 3 egg whites
1.25 ml (¼ tsp) lemon juice
450 g (1 lb) icing sugar, sifted
5 ml (1 tsp) glycerine

1 Place the egg whites and lemon juice in a clean bowl. Stir to break up the egg whites.

2 Add a little icing sugar and mix well to form the consistency of unwhipped cream. Continue mixing and adding small quantities of icing sugar every few minutes until the desired consistency has been reached, mixing well and beating gently after each addition. The icing should be smooth, glossy and light, almost like a cold meringue in texture, but not aerated. Do not add the icing sugar too quickly or it will produce a dull, heavy icing. Stir in the glycerine until well blended.

3 Alternatively, for large quantities of royal icing use a food mixer on the lowest speed, following the instructions above.

4 Allow the icing to settle before use; cover the surface with a piece of damp cling film and seal well, excluding all the air.

5 Stir the icing thoroughly before using it as this will disperse the air bubbles, then adjust the consistency if necessary by adding more sifted icing sugar.

READY-TO-ROLL ICING

This icing, sometimes called sugarpaste, is widely available in supermarkets and is incredibly easy to use. I have not given a recipe for sugarpaste as it is so much more convenient to buy it. When rolling the icing out, first dust your work surface with a little sifted cornflour to prevent sticking. Add more cornflour as you work if necessary. See the instructions for covering a cake with ready-to-roll icing on page 13.

BUTTER CREAM

75 g (3 oz) unsalted butter, softened
175 g (6 oz) icing sugar, sifted
a few drops of vanilla essence
15-30 ml (1-2 tbsp) milk or water

1 Put the butter in a bowl and beat with a wooden spoon until it is light and fluffy.

2 Gradually stir in the icing sugar, vanilla and milk or water. Beat well until light and smooth.

VARIATIONS

Orange, lime or lemon – Replace the vanilla essence with a little finely grated orange, lime or lemon rind. Add a little juice from the fruit instead of the milk, beating well to avoid curdling the mixture. If the mixture is to be piped, omit the fruit rinds.

Coffee – Replace the vanilla essence with 10 ml (2 tsp) instant coffee granules dissolved in 15 ml (1 tbsp) boiling water; cool before adding to the mixture.

Chocolate – Blend 15 ml (1 tbsp) cocoa powder with 30 ml (2 tbsp) boiling water and cool before adding to the mixture.

MARZIPAN

125 g (4 oz) icing sugar, sifted
125 g (4 oz) caster sugar
225 g (8 oz) ground almonds
5 ml (1 tsp) lemon juice
a few drops of almond essence
1 egg or 2 egg yolks, beaten

1 Put the sugars and almonds in a large bowl.

2 Add the lemon juice, almond essence and enough egg to make a firm but manageable dough.

3 Turn the marzipan on to a work surface dusted with sifted icing sugar and knead with your hands until smooth.

4 The marzipan may be used for modelling in place of ready-to-roll icing (see pages 18–19).

MOULDED FIGURES

When moulding figures, marzipan is used for figures that need to be sturdy and stand upright. It is firm and easy to work. Ready-to-roll icing is used for delicate figures and finer work. The animals in this section can be made with either material. However, figures like the wrestler must be made from marzipan.

SUGAR MOUSE

1 Roll white icing into a pear shape for the body. Roll two small balls and flatten them for the ears. Snip whiskers using scissors.

2 Roll two small balls of pink ready-to-roll icing and flatten them. Attach them to the white ears with a little water. Pinch the base together and press into the mouse at either side of the head using a cocktail stick.

3 Attach the tail with a little water. Pipe the eyes.

DUCK

1 Roll orange marzipan or ready-to-roll icing into a small pear shape with a long thin end. Take a marble-size piece of yellow or white, roll it into a ball, then press between the thumb and forefinger to make the head. Roll the head on to the beak.

2 Use the rest of the yellow or white to make an elongated pear shape. Tip the pointed end of the pear upwards to make a duck's tail.

3 Attach the head to the body with a little royal icing and pipe eyes on the head using white then black royal icing.

RABBIT

1 Roll ready-to-roll icing into a pear shape. Using a small pair of scissors, snip two ears from the pointed end.

2 Using a little royal icing, pipe eyes in white then black and a big round white tail.

STANDING KITTEN

1 Reserve a marble-size piece of marzipan or ready-to-roll icing for the head and roll the rest into a sausage about 7.5 cm (3 inches) long. Make a 2 cm (³/₄ inch) cut at each end of the sausage to form the front and back legs. Mark claws with a sharp knife. Arch the sausage so that it will stand up. Snip a tail from the back.

2 Make the head in the same way as the Sitting Kitten and attach the head with royal icing. Pipe white and black eyes and a pink nose using royal icing.

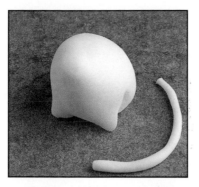

SITTING KITTEN

1 Roll a marble-size piece of marzipan or ready-to-roll icing into a ball and flatten it a little. Make a cut one-third of the way through the top and ease each side into ears. Snip whiskers each side of the face.

2 Roll a length for the tail and the rest into a pear shape for the body. Stand it on end and cut two front paws from the bottom slightly tipping the body forward.

3 Use a little royal icing to attach the tail to the back, curling it around. Attach the head to the body and pipe white and black eyes and a pink nose.

WRESTLING FIGURE

Use 50 g (2 oz) flesh-coloured marzipan and 50 g (2 oz) coloured marzipan for each figure. Dry for 3-4 days.

1 Roll a ball of marzipan for the head. Roll a long sausage for the arms and use your little finger to shape the muscles. Flatten each end for the hands and score fingers. Roll out two legs, marking the muscles.

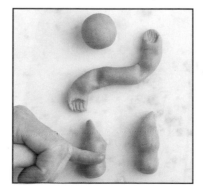

2 Divide the coloured marzipan in half. Shape one piece into the trunk of the body making a 'V' shape where the legs will join. Reserve a small piece of the remaining coloured marzipan for the straps of the wrestler's suit, wrap lightly and store in an airtight container. Divide the rest into two and shape into boots, matching the width of the legs where they will join. Make sure they are quite thin and flat so that the figure will stand up.

3 Firmly press the arms to the top of the body. Cut the tops of the legs at an angle and press on to the base of the body. Press the boots on to the legs. Carefully place on non-stick baking parchment to dry.

4 To assemble the figure, roll out the reserved coloured marzipan thinly and cut straps for the wrestler's suit. Place over the shoulders. Paint the eyes and a mouth. Use piped royal icing for the hair or press some marzipan through a sieve on to the head. Attach the head to the body with icing.

The

CAKES

PAINTBOX

Filling the holes in the top of this cake with even-sized pieces of coloured icing makes a really effective 'paint palette', perfect for any creative child.

Victoria sandwich cake mixture made with 175 g (6 oz) flour (see page 14)

½ quantity butter cream (see page 16)

35 x 25 cm (14 x 10 inch) rectangular board or tray

1 kg (2 lb 4 oz) ready-to-roll icing

blue, yellow, pink, black, red and green food colourings

1 Make the cake mixture, turn into a prepared 28 × 18 cm (11 × 7 inch) rectangular shallow tin and bake for 25-30 minutes until just firm. Turn out, remove the lining paper and place on a wire rack to cool.

2 Colour 325 g (11 oz) of the ready-to-roll icing dark blue, 15 g (½ oz) light blue, 35 g (1¼ oz) yellow, 35 g (1¼ oz) pink, 35 g (1¼ oz) black, 15 g (½ oz) red, 15 g (½ oz) dark green and 15 g (½ oz) light green, leaving the remainder white.

3 Invert the cake so the base is uppermost and cut out a long, deep groove from the centre, almost to the ends of the sponge. Position on the board and spread with the butter cream.

4 Roll out three-quarters of the white icing the same size as the base of the cake (use the tin as a guide if liked) and position on the cake. Using a 5 cm (2 inch) round cutter, cut out eight circles from the top of the cake, using a twisting action so the icing doesn't become too displaced.

5 Roll out the dark blue icing thickly and cut out long thin strips 3 cm (1¼ inches) wide. Use to cover the sides of the cake.

6 Take 15 g (½ oz) balls of each of the icing colours. Roll each into a neat ball shape and flatten to a 5 cm (2 inch) round. Use to fill in the holes on top of the cake. Roll out the white icing thinly and cut out shapes to resemble paper. Arrange on the cake board, securing them with a dampened paintbrush and cutting them to fit around the box and edges of the board or tray.

7 Use the remaining coloured icings to shape two paintbrushes, each about 16 cm (6¼ inches) long. Arrange one in the box and one on the board. Dilute two or three of the food colourings and paint lines on to the white icing.

HINT
Instead of abstract lines, paint a birthday or other message on to the white icing on the cake board instead.

FLUFFY SHEEP

Simply swirled with royal icing, this is one of the simplest cakes to decorate. Any young child will fall in love with this friendly little sheep.

Madeira cake mixture made with 125 g (4 oz) plain flour (see pages 14–15)

½ quantity butter cream (see page 16)

25 cm (10 inch) round cake board

250 g (9 oz) ready-to-roll icing

brown, green and black food colourings

1 quantity royal icing (see page 16)

---

1 Make the cake mixture, turn into a prepared 3.4 litre (6 pint) ovenproof bowl and bake for about 1¼ hours until just firm. Leave to cool in the bowl, then loosen the edges with a palette knife to ease the cake out of the bowl.

2 Cut off any dome from the top of the cake, then split the cake horizontally into three layers. Sandwich together with all but 30 ml (2 tbsp) of the butter cream and place on the cake board. Spread with the remaining butter cream.

3 Colour 150 g (5 oz) of the ready-to-roll icing brown and the rest green, leaving a small ball of white. Roll out the green icing thinly and use to cover the cake board. Trim off the excess icing.

4 Spread the royal icing all over the cake in an even layer, then swirl lightly with the tip of a knife. Roll two-thirds of the brown icing into a ball and flatten into an oval shape. Press gently on to the top of the cake. From the remaining brown icing, shape two small ears and two front feet; press into the icing. (If necessary, prop the ears on balls of crumpled foil until they set.)

5 Make two eyes in white icing and secure in position with a dampened paintbrush. Using the black food colouring and a fine paintbrush, paint the features.

HINT
If you don't have a suitable large ovenproof mixing bowl, use an 18 cm (7 inch) round tin and round off the top edge.

HAPPY HOUSE

This is a fun house with cheerful, smiling features that any small child will warm to.

Madeira cake mixture made with 175 g (6 oz) plain flour (see pages 14-15)

1 quantity butter cream (see page 16)

jam, for filling

1.3 kg (2³/₄ lb) ready-to-roll icing

pink, green, red, yellow and blue food colourings

23 cm (9 inch) square cake board

1 Make the cake mixture and turn into a prepared 18 cm (7 inch) square cake tin. Bake for about 1¹/₂ hours, or until the cake springs back when lightly pressed in the centre. Leave to cool in the tin, then turn out and leave on a wire rack to cool completely.

2 Cut the cake in half vertically. Slice off the domed top of one half and position the other half on top. Cut a slanting slice off the short ends so the cake is slightly narrower at the base. Halve the two cakes horizontally then sandwich the layers back together with two-thirds of the butter cream and the jam.

3 Colour 500 g (1 lb 2 oz) of the icing pink, 275 g (9 oz) green, 300 g (11 oz) red, 50 g (2 oz) yellow and 25 g (1 oz) blue. Leave the remainder white.

4 Dampen the cake board with water. Roll out 175 g (6 oz) of the green icing thinly and use to cover the board, trimming off the excess around the edges. Position the cake near the back of the board and spread with the remaining butter cream.

5 Measure the sides of the cake and roll out the pink icing to fit. Wrap the icing around the sides of the cake and smooth down gently. Roll out 250 g (9 oz) red icing to a 21 × 10 cm (8¹/₄ × 4 inch) rectangle and score lengthways with a knife. Lay over the top of the cake. From the red trimmings, cut a curved strip and position on the front of the cake, under the roof, using a dampened paintbrush to secure it. Use the remaining red icing to make a small chimney and curved door. (See template on page 92).

6 Use the white icing to make two windows and a front path, marking window panes with a knife. Use blue icing for the dots on the path and to cover one pane in each window. Use yellow icing to shape sills over the windows. Roll out the remaining yellow icing thinly and cut 2 cm ³/₄ inch) wide strips. Use to shape a ribbon in front of the chimney.

7 Roll different sized balls of the remaining green icing and taper them into cone shaped trees. Arrange them in front of the house.

HINT

For additional decorations, make small flowers using the icing trimmings or stick candles in the cake board 'garden'.

KITTEN CASTLE

The perfect cake for a little girl. The combination of meringue
and sponge will be very popular.

**Victoria sandwich cake
mixture made with 350 g
(12 oz) flour
(see page 14)**

**1½ quantities butter
cream (see page 16)**

pink food colouring

strawberry jam, for filling

**25-28 cm (10-11 inch)
cake board (optional)**

TURRETS

2 egg whites

125 g (4 oz) caster sugar

hundreds and thousands

DECORATION

flat sweets, for windows

**1 sitting kitten
(see pages 18-19)**

1 Collect three empty food cans
to bake the turrets in: one 450 g
(1 lb) size, one 225 g (8 oz) size
and one 150 g (5 oz) size. Use a
20.5 cm (8 inch) round cake tin
for the castle base. Grease and
base line all the tins.

2 Make the cake mixture. Half fill
the food cans with the mixture
and turn the rest into the cake
tin. Bake the small cakes for 20-30
minutes and the large cake for 1
hour. Turn out, remove the lining
papers and leave to cool on a
wire rack.

3 To make the meringue turrets,
reduce the oven temperature to
110°C (225°F) Mark ¼. Line a
baking sheet with non-stick baking
parchment. Draw three circles on
the parchment using the food
cans as a guide. Whisk the egg
whites until stiff. Gradually whisk
in half the sugar, whisking after
each addition until thoroughly
incorporated. Then fold in the
remaining sugar very lightly, with a
metal spoon.

4 Spoon the meringue into a
piping bag fitted with a large star
nozzle. Pipe three large whirls of
meringue, starting outside the
circles so that the meringue will
overlap the edge of the turrets.
Sprinkle the tops with hundreds
and thousands. Pipe the remaining
meringue into tiny stars. Bake the
star meringues for 1-1½ hours
and the turrets for 3 hours until
firm and crisp. Cool on a wire
rack. Store in an airtight container
until required.

5 To assemble the cake, first
colour the butter cream pink. Slice
the large cake in half and

sandwich together with the
strawberry jam. Set the cake on
the board, if using, or a serving
plate and cover the top and sides
with butter cream. Carefully coat
each turret with butter cream,
inserting a fork into an end so the
cake can be iced more easily. Set
each turret on top of the cake.

6 Press sweets on to the sides of
the turrets for windows and
arrange the small meringue stars
around the side of the large cake.
Set a large meringue on top of
each turret. Put the kitten in place
on the cake.

SHAPE SORTER

Most very young children have a shape sorter in their toy cupboard.
This simple cake is ideal for a first birthday celebration.

Victoria sandwich cake mixture made with 175 g (6 oz) flour (see page 14)

jam, for filling

½ quantity butter cream (see page 16)

25 cm (10 inch) round cake board

yellow, red, blue and green food colourings

1 kg (2 lb 4 oz) ready-to-roll icing

---

1 Make the cake mixture and turn into two prepared 18 cm (7 inch) sandwich tins. Bake for about 25-30 minutes, until the cakes are well risen and spring back when lightly pressed. Turn out, remove the lining paper and cool on a wire rack.

2 Sandwich the cakes with the jam and all but 45 ml (3 tbsp) of the butter cream. Colour 375 g (13 oz) of the ready-to-roll icing yellow, 325 g (11 oz) red, 200 g (7 oz) blue and 75 g (3 oz) green.

3 Roll out 175 g (6 oz) of the yellow icing thinly and use to cover the cake board. Position the cake on the board, slightly to one side and spread with the reserved butter cream. Roll out 125 g (4 oz) of the blue icing to an 18 cm (7 inch) round and use to cover the top of the cake. Leave to set overnight.

4 Measure the circumference of the cake using a piece of string. Roll out 250 g (9 oz) of the red icing to a long thin strip and cut to the length of the string and the depth of the cake. Secure around the cake and smooth into place.

5 Roll out two-thirds of the yellow icing to an 18 cm (7 inch) round and lay on top of the cake over the blue icing, trimming off any excess around the edges. Using cutters, cut out shapes from the yellow icing and lift out the cut-out icing to reveal the blue .

6 Dampen the top edge of the red icing with water. Roll out the remaining yellow icing to a long strip, 2 cm (¾ inch) wide and the length of the string. Secure around the top edge of the cake.

7 Roll out the remaining blue, red and green icing to about 1.5 cm (⅝ inch) thick and cut out shapes using the same cutters. Leave to dry on a piece of greaseproof paper, then arrange on the cake and cake board.

HINT

If you don't have a selection of cutters, use the templates on page 93.

FIRST TELEPHONE

For tots who love traditional-style telephone toys with finger dials,
this cake is the perfect birthday treat.

**Madeira cake mixture
made with 125 g (4 oz)
plain flour
(see pages 14–15)**

**¹/₂ quantity butter cream
(see page 16)**

jam, for filling

**800 g (1 lb 12 oz) ready-
to-roll icing**

**yellow, blue and red food
colourings**

**20.5 cm (8 inch) square
cake board**

5 Smarties

1 Make the cake mixture and turn into a prepared 15 cm (6 inch) square cake tin. Bake for about 1¹/₄ hours, or until the cake springs back when lightly pressed in the centre. Leave to cool in the tin then turn out and leave on a wire rack to cool completely.

2 Cut a small sloping wedge from the cake, finishing about 2 cm (³/₄ inch) down one side, then cut off 1 cm (¹/₂ inch) from the two opposite sides. Halve the cake horizontally and sandwich with half the butter cream and the jam.

3 Colour 400 g (14 oz) of the ready-to-roll icing yellow, 125 g (4 oz) very light blue, 75 g (3 oz) dark blue and 200 g (7 oz) red, leaving a tiny ball of white for the eyes. Dampen the cake board with water. Roll out the light blue icing thinly and use to cover the board, trimming off the excess around the edges. Position the cake on the board and spread with the remaining butter cream.

4 Roll out the yellow icing and use to cover the cake. Smooth it to fit around the sides and trim off the excess around the base. Roll 150 g (5 oz) of the red icing into a thick sausage, 16 cm (6¹/₄ inches) long. Dampen the highest point of the yellow icing with water and position the red icing for the receiver, smoothing it down lightly.

5 Cut out a 9 cm (3¹/₂ inch) circle from the remaining red icing, then press out small holes using a small cutter or wide end of a piping nozzle. Secure to the telephone and press a Smartie into the centre. Use the white icing to shape two eyes and position above the dial, adding blue centres and small eyebrows from the red trimmings.

6 Divide the remaining blue icing into four pieces and shape into wheels. Secure at the sides of the cake and press a Smartie into the centre of each. If you like, finish the cake by writing the child's name and age on the dial.

TOADSTOOL

This cake will really capture the imaginations of young children who believe in woodland fairies.

Victoria sandwich cake mixture made with 175 g (6 oz) flour (see page 14)

700 g (1½ lb) ready-to-roll icing

brown, red, green, yellow and black food colourings

½ quantity butter cream (see page 16)

dolly mixtures and liquorice allsorts

a little royal icing (see page 16)

---

1 Grease and base line a 900 g (2 lb) food can and a 1.1 litre (2 pint) pudding basin. Make the cake mixture, half fill the food can and turn the remaining mixture into the pudding basin. Bake at 190°C (375°F) Mark 5 for about 30 minutes for the food can and about 40 minutes for the pudding basin. Turn out, remove the lining paper and cool on a wire rack.

2 Take 350 g (12 oz) of the ready-to-roll icing. Colour a walnut-sized piece beige and the rest a not too bright red. Colour 125 g (4 oz) of the remaining icing green and leave the rest white. Roll out the green icing and cut into a kidney shape as 'grass'. Fix to cake board or serving plate with a little water. Using the food can that the 'stalk' was baked in, cut a semicircle from one side of the 'grass'.

3 Reserve 50 g (2 oz) of the white icing and roll out the rest as wide as the 'stalk' and long enough to fit all the way round. (Measure the circumference with a piece of string first.) Trim to neaten the edges. Spread butter cream thinly round the cake. Holding the cake by the ends, set it at one end of the rolled out icing. Roll up and press the seam together. With a dab of butter cream, fix it upright into the semicircle cut out of the green icing. Spread the uncovered top with butter cream.

4 Roll out the red icing to fit the pudding basin cake. Set the cake flat on the work surface and cover thinly with butter cream. Lay the icing over the cake smoothly. Trim the edges to the base of the cake. Dust the work surface with cornflour and carefully turn the cake upside-down.

5 Colour the remaining butter cream yellow and put into a piping bag fitted with a small fluted nozzle. Mark a circle where the stalk will fit on the centre of the cake. Pipe lines of butter cream on the underneath, starting at the mark you have made, to look like the 'gills' of a toadstool. Make sure you cover the sponge and icing join. Carefully turn the cake the right way up and set on top of the stalk.

6 Roll out the reserved white icing and the beige icing. Cut the white icing into dots. Using a little water to secure them, arrange over the top of the toadstool. Cut the beige icing into a door and windows and attach to the stalk.

7 Make some sweetie insects. The ones in the picture are a caterpillar of assorted dolly mixtures and piped eyes; a snail made from three liquorice allsorts stuck together with royal icing, with piped eyes and sliced liquorice allsort for antennae; and a bug made from a sliced liquorice allsort with piped eyes. Use the red icing trimmings, rolled into small ovals, to make ladybird candle holders. Put the black royal icing in a bag fitted with a medium writing nozzle. Pipe dots and eyes on the ladybirds, a doorknob on the door and panes on the windows.

BALL PIT

This cake is much easier to make than it appears. Once the face and limbs are positioned, you simply surround them with icing balls.

Victoria sandwich cake mixture made with 225 g (8 oz) flour (see page 14)

1 quantity butter cream (see page 16)

jam, for filling

25 cm (10 inch) round cake board

red, flesh-coloured (if available), green, yellow and blue food colourings

1 kg (2 lb 4 oz) ready-to-roll icing

wooden cocktail sticks

---

1 Make the cake mixture and turn into the two prepared 20.5 cm (8 inch) round sandwich tins. Bake for about 30 minutes or until just firm to touch. Turn out and leave to cool on a wire rack.

2 Sandwich the cakes with half the butter cream and the jam and place on the cake board. Spread with the remaining butter cream.

3 Colour 650 g (1 lb 7 oz) of the ready-to-roll icing red and 100 g (3½ oz) flesh coloured (see Hint). Reserve a small piece of white icing for the socks. Colour 100 g (3½ oz) blue, then divide the remainder into two and colour green and yellow.

4 Roll out 150 g (5 oz) of the red icing and use to cover the top of the cake. Measure the circumference of the cake using a piece of string. Roll out the remaining red icing to a long strip, the length of the string and 5 mm (¼ inch) deeper than the cake. Wrap it around the sides of the cake so the icing stands proud around the top, fitting the ends neatly together and smoothing down gently. Roll out some blue icing thinly and use to cover the edges of the cake board, trimming off the excess.

5 Roll 50 g (2 oz) of the flesh-coloured icing into a ball and secure to the top of the cake with a dampened paintbrush for the head. From the remaining flesh-coloured icing, shape two forearms and legs. Push a cocktail stick into each limb, then press them down, at a slight angle into the cake. Shape the white icing into socks and secure to the legs. Roll a very thin strip of yellow icing and cut slits along one edge. Wrap around the head for hair.

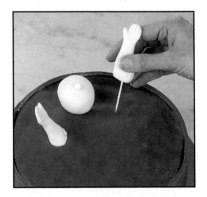

6 Use the remaining icing to shape the balls. To make sure they're evenly sized, roll out each colour under the palms of your hands into long ropes and cut at regular lengths, then roll into balls and scatter on top of the cake.

7 Shape and position tiny balls of white for the eyes. Paint the features using a fine paintbrush and food colouring.

HINT
If you cannot find flesh-coloured food colouring, use a dash of red colouring in its place but be very careful not to use too much.

PANDA BEAR

Animals - particularly those of the cuddly variety - are popular with children of all ages. This contented panda sits on a dome-shaped base, made by baking the cake in a pudding basin.

Victoria sandwich cake mixture made with 175 g (6 oz) flour (see page 14)

²/₃ quantity orange-flavoured butter cream (see page 16)

18 cm (7 inch) round cake board

60 ml (4 tbsp) apricot glaze (see page 16)

1.4 kg (3 lb) ready-to-roll icing

dark and light green, brown, yellow and black food colourings

15 ml (1 tbsp) lightly beaten egg white

about 125 g (4 oz) icing sugar

1 Grease and base line a 1.4 litre (2¹/₂ pint) pudding basin. Make the cake mixture and turn into the prepared basin. Bake in the oven at 190°C (375°F) Mark 5 for about 45 minutes. Leave to cool in the pudding basin.

2 Trim the cake so that it sits flat when inverted. Slice the cake horizontally into three layers and sandwich together with the butter cream. Then place the cake on the cake board and brush all over with apricot glaze.

3 Colour 700 g (1¹/₂ lb) of the ready-to-roll icing dark green. Roll it out to a 25 cm (10 inch) round. Use to cover the cake, easing the icing around the side to eliminate creases and folds. Trim off the excess icing at the base and reserve the trimmings.

4 To make the panda, roll 225 g (8 oz) icing into a ball for the body. Stand it on the work surface and elongate the top of the ball slightly. Roll another 50 g (2 oz) for the head and secure to body, using a dampened paintbrush. Pinch the front of the head to a point to make a snout. Use another 25 g (1 oz) for each leg and 15 g (¹/₂ oz) for each arm. Shape and secure. Use a little more icing to shape ears and secure to the head.

5 Beat the egg white in a bowl, gradually adding the icing sugar until softly peaking. Lightly dampen the panda and brush with the icing to make fur. Reserve the remaining icing. Place a dampened piece of cling film directly on to the surface of the icing to prevent it drying out.

6 Colour half the ready-to-roll icing different shades of green, a quarter brown and a quarter yellow. Roll out each colour separately and cut out small leaf shapes between 2.5 cm (1 inch) and 5 cm (2 inches) long. Lay the leaves over a foil-covered rolling pin and wooden spoon. Make a small brown twig and set everything aside, with the panda, for 24 hours to set.

7 Paint the panda with black food colouring. Secure a few small leaves on to the brown twig. Position the panda on the cake. Place a little icing in a piping bag fitted with a fine writing nozzle and use to pipe claws. Colour the remaining icing green and use to secure the leaves around the panda and cake board.

HINT

Most children like chocolate cake, so flavour the cake mixture if liked (see page 14). Chocolate goes very well with the orange-flavoured butter cream.

BIRD HOUSE

This cake, showing three little birds snuggled up in a cosy bird house safe from the snow, is lovely for any winter birthday.

Madeira cake mixture made with 125 g (4 oz) plain flour (see pages 14–15)

1 quantity butter cream (see page 16)

jam, for filling

1.1 kg (2 lb 8 oz) ready-to-roll icing

green, brown, red, yellow, orange and blue food colourings

23 cm (9 inch) round cake board

1 shredded wheat

1 Grease and base line a 23 cm (9 inch) cake tin. Make the cake mixture and turn into the prepared tin. Bake for about 1¼ hours, or until the cake springs back when lightly pressed in the centre. Leave to cool in the tin.

2 Cut off the dome from the top of the cake then cut the cake vertically into quarters. Use half the butter cream and all the jam to sandwich the cakes together into a stack.

3 Cut off two wedges from the top sponge to shape a roof. Press a 7.5 cm (3 inch) cutter into one end of the house. Remove it and scoop out about 2.5 cm (1 inch) depth of sponge.

4 Colour 125 g (4 oz) of the icing green, 500 g (1 lb 2 oz) brown, 250 g (9 oz) red, 50 g (2 oz) yellow and 15 g (½ oz) orange, leaving the remainder white.

5 Dampen the cake board with water. Roll out the green icing thinly and use to cover the board, trimming off the excess around the edges. Position the cake on the board and spread with the remaining butter cream.

6 Roll out the brown icing and use to cover the sides of the bird house, one side at a time. Mark the horizontal lines using the back of a knife. Use the brown icing trimmings to line the hole in the cake. Dampen the icing in the hole. Break up the shredded wheat and press it into the soft icing to secure.

7 For the roof, roll out the red icing to a 15 × 13 cm (6 × 5 inch) rectangle. Position on top of the cake with the longer sides at the front and back of the cake. Smooth down gently.

8 Roll the yellow icing into three small balls for the birds' heads. Snip the tops with scissors. Cut out three orange diamond shapes and fold in half for the beaks. Press into position. Add small balls of white for the eyes. Secure the birds on blobs of icing trimmings.

9 Roll out half the white icing to a 10 cm (4 inch) circle with a wavy edge. Secure to the roof. From the rest cut out a long thin strip with a wavy edge. Fix around the edges of the board. Use food colouring and a fine paintbrush to paint the birds' features.

ROBOT

A quick and easy cake to make for a young child. The children will enjoy the colourful decoration of sweets too!

Victoria sandwich cake mixture made with 175 g (6 oz) flour (see page 14)

½ quantity butter cream (see page 16)

jam, for filling (optional)

20.5 cm (8 inch) round cake board (optional)

black and yellow food colourings

1 round biscuit (any sort will do)

25 g (1 oz) ready-to-roll icing

1 tube of Smarties

1 packet of Jelly Tots

1 packet of fruit Polos

3 lollipops

---

1 Grease and base line a 1.1 litre (2 pint) pudding basin, a 300 ml (½ pint) pudding basin and a bun tin (or use a paper fairy cake case). Make the cake mixture and spoon into the prepared basins and bun tin. Bake in the oven at 190°C (375°F) Mark 5. Bake the smaller cakes for 20-30 minutes and the large one for about 45-60 minutes. Turn out, remove the lining papers and leave to cool on a wire rack.

2 Slice the large cake in half and sandwich together with jam, if using, or some of the butter cream. Set the large cake on the cake board, if using, or serving plate. Attach the small cake to the top with a little butter cream. Colour the rest of the butter cream pale grey and use to cover the cake completely.

3 Attach the bun to the biscuit with butter cream, then spread butter cream on top of the bun. Colour the ready-to-roll icing yellow and roll out thinly. Use to cover the bun and biscuit.

4 Arrange rows of Smarties on the lower half of the cake and two for the eyes. Arrange the Jelly Tots around the join between the head and base of the robot. Put the yellow covered bun on top. Thread three fruit Polos on to a lolly stick and push into the top of the robot. Do the same with the other two lollies and push into the cake at the front.

HINT

The birthday child's favourite sweets may be used to decorate the cake.

IN THE SWIM

This is a lovely cake for young children who enjoy splashing around in the swimming pool.

Victoria sandwich cake mixture made with 225 g (8 oz) flour (see page 14)

1 quantity butter cream (see page 16)

jam, for filling

25 cm (10 inch) round cake board

1 kg (2 lb 4 oz) ready-to-roll icing

blue, flesh-coloured (if available), orange and yellow food colourings

1 Make the cake mixture and turn into two prepared 20.5 cm (8 inch) round sandwich tins. Bake for about 30 minutes until just firm to the touch. Turn out, remove the lining paper and leave to cool on a wire rack.

2 Sandwich the cakes with half the butter cream and the jam and place on the cake board. Reserve 30 ml (2 tbsp) of the remaining butter cream, then spread the remainder over the cake.

3 Colour 650 g (1 lb 7 oz) of the ready-to-roll icing light blue, 150 g (5 oz) dark blue, 100 g (3½ oz) flesh coloured (see Hint on page 36), 75 g (3 oz) orange and 15 g (½ oz) yellow.

4 Roll out the light blue icing and use to cover the cake, smoothing it to fit around the sides. Trim off the excess icing around the base. Roll out the orange icing thinly and use to cover the edges of the cake board, trimming off the excess.

5 Roll the dark blue icing into a ball and flatten it out neatly to a 9 cm (3½ inch) round. Use a 5.5 cm (2¼ inch) cutter to cut out the centre. Round off the cut edge with your fingers and place the ring on top of the cake. Roll tiny balls of the orange trimmings and yellow icing and flatten them between your thumb and finger. Secure to the blue ring with a dampened paintbrush.

6 Roll 25 g (1 oz) of the flesh-coloured icing into an oval shape and fit inside the ring. Roll another 35 g (1½ oz) into a ball and position for the head. Use a tiny dot of icing for the nose. Roll the remainder into a sausage shape and cut in half. Curve into shape for the girl's arms and position on the cake.

7 Put the reserved butter cream in a piping bag fitted with a writing nozzle and use to pipe hair over the head. Use the remaining butter cream to pipe wavy lines around the ring and to pipe 'bubbles' on the sides of the cake. Paint the facial features using food colouring and a fine paintbrush.

HINT

If you are making this cake for a little boy, make the swimmer in the ring male.

PINK PIG

This is a really fun cake for any animal lover. To achieve a good shape you'll need to cover the cake with a thin layer of icing and leave it to set overnight, before covering with a second layer.

Madeira cake mixture made with 175 g (6 oz) plain flour (see pages 14–15)

1 quantity butter cream (see page 00)

jam, for filling

1.25 kg (2 lb 12 oz) ready-to-roll icing

red, pink and black food colourings

23 cm (9 inch) round cake board

1 Grease and base line two 600 ml (1 pint) ovenproof bowls with greaseproof paper. Make the cake mixture, turn into the bowls and level the surfaces. Bake for about 50 minutes or until just firm. Leave to cool in the bowls, then loosen the edges with a palette knife and ease the cake out of the bowls. Colour 150 g (5 oz) of the ready-to-roll icing red and the remainder pink.

2 Cut the domes off the top of the cakes. Halve each cake horizontally. Sandwich each cake with butter cream and jam, then sandwich the two cakes together with more butter cream and jam.

3 Dampen the cake board with water. Roll out the red icing and use to cover the board, trimming off the excess around the edges.

4 Roll out just under half of the pink icing to a 33 cm (13 inch) round and lay it over the cake. Ease the icing around the sides, trimming to fit in an even layer. (Don't worry too much about the finish, as the cake will have a second layer of icing.) Smooth the icing down with the palms of your hands and leave to set overnight in a cool place.

5 Transfer the cake to the cake board. Reserve 150 g (5 oz) of the remaining pink icing. Roll out the rest to a round as before and use to cover the cake in a second layer, this time trimming and smoothing out as many joins as possible.

6 Roll a little icing into a ball and flatten into a 'snout'. Secure to the front of the cake and make two nostrils using the end of a paintbrush. Shape four small balls of icing for feet and make a deep cut into each. Position on the cake.

7 Shape two large flat ears and small curly tail and secure in place. Paint the eyes and mouth using black food colouring and a fine paintbrush.

RED BUS

For many young children who usually travel in cars, going on a bus ride is a real treat. This 'double-decker' is the next best thing.

Madeira cake mixture made with 175 g (6 oz) plain flour (see pages 14–15)

1 quantity butter cream (see page 16)

jam, for filling

1 kg (2 lb 4 oz) ready-to-roll icing

red, black, blue, yellow and silver food colourings

25 cm (10 inch) round cake board

1 candy or chocolate stick

4 liquorice Catherine wheels

1 Make the cake mixture and turn into a prepared 18 cm (7 inch) square cake tin. Bake for about 1½ hours or until the cake springs back when pressed gently in the centre.

2 Slice the dome off the top of the cake and halve the cake, first horizontally, then vertically. Stack the rectangles of cake on top of one another, sandwiching the layers with half the butter cream and the jam. Using a small knife, cut out a square from the front of the cake for the area next to the driver's cab and another at the back left-hand side of the cake.

3 Colour 650 g (1 lb 7 oz) of the icing red, 200 g (7 oz) grey, 100 g (3½ oz) light blue, 15 g (½ oz) yellow and 15 g (½ oz) black, leaving the rest white. Lightly dampen the cake board. Roll out the grey icing thinly and use to cover the cake board, trimming off the excess. Place the cake on the board and spread with the remaining butter cream.

4 Roll out the red icing and use to cover the cake, one side at a time, finishing with the cut-out areas at the back and front. Once all the sections are covered, smooth out the icing with the palms of your hands.

5 Shape a small square of black icing and use to cover the base of the platform at the back. Trim the candy or chocolate stick to the right length and push into position.

6 Roll out the blue icing thinly and cut into rectangles. Secure around the cake for the windows. From the yellow and white icing, shape and position the radiator, bus number plate, route number plate, headlights and road markings.

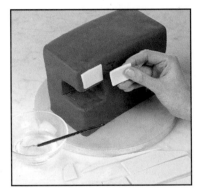

7 Unroll the liquorice wheels until they're a suitable size for the bus wheels. Secure to the sides with blobs of red icing trimmings.

8 Using a paintbrush and silver food colouring, paint the radiator and edges of the headlights. Write the child's name on the bus number plate and age on the route number plate. Dilute a little black or blue food colouring and use to scribble faint lines over the windows.

ANIMAL CAROUSEL

This is a spectacular cake for girls or a little boy, made using sponge, meringue and marshmallow.

Lemon-flavoured Victoria sponge cake mixture made with 275 g (10 oz) flour (see page 14)

lemon curd, for filling

700 g (1½ lb) ready-to-roll icing

pink, purple and yellow food colourings

30 ml (2 tbsp) clear honey

a little royal icing (see page 16)

5 satay sticks

5 marshmallow twists or straws

5 moulded animals (see pages 18–19)

MERINGUE

2 egg whites

125 g (4 oz) caster sugar

1 Make the cake mixture and turn into a prepared 20.5 cm (8 inch) round cake tin. Bake for 1 hour. Turn out, remove the lining paper and cool on a wire rack.

2 To make the meringue reduce the oven to 110°C (225°F) Mark ¼. Line a baking sheet with non-stick baking parchment. Draw a 20.5 cm (8 inch) round on the paper. Whisk the egg whites until stiff. Gradually whisk in half the sugar, until incorporated.

3 Fold in the remaining sugar very lightly with a metal spoon. Colour the meringue pink. Spoon into a piping bag fitted with 1 cm (½ inch) plain nozzle. Pipe in rings to fill the circle. Separately pipe a whirl for the centre of the canopy and five tiny meringues. Bake for about 1½ hours until dry.

4 Slice the cake in half and fill with lemon curd. Colour one-third of the ready-to-roll icing lilac and the rest lemon. Make a template: cut a 25 cm (10 inch) round from greaseproof paper. Fold the paper into sixteenths then draw a semicircle at the bottom edge and cut out. Open up the paper and you will have a circle with a scalloped edge.

5 Add 15 ml (1 tbsp) water to the honey and heat until boiling. Roll out the lilac icing into a long strip to fit around the side of the cake. Brush the side with the honey and, holding the cake upright, roll the sides on to the icing. Set on a board or serving plate; smooth over the seam.

6 Roll out the lemon-coloured icing into a circle. Cut out using the template as a guide. Brush the top and edge of the cake with hot honey. Put the lemon-coloured icing over the top and smooth down.

7 Colour the royal icing pink and put into a piping bag fitted with a fine star nozzle. Pipe shells and dots around the lilac cake sides.

8 Push the satay sticks through the marshmallows and attach to the cake at evenly spaced points. Trim the tops. Pipe royal icing on top of each 'pole' and secure the meringue canopy on top.

9 Attach the large meringue in the centre and the baby ones over the top of each pole. Place the animals on the cake.

SLEEPY RAG DOLL

Here's a cake for a dreamer. This little rag doll is sound asleep. Do you think she should be woken up?

Madeira cake mixture made with 125 g (4 oz) plain flour (see pages 14–15)

1 quantity butter cream (see page 16)

jam, for filling

800 g (1 lb 12 oz) ready-to-roll icing

brown, red, green and yellow food colourings

25 cm (10 inch) round cake board

1 Grease and line a 900 g (2 lb) loaf tin. Make the cake mixture and turn into the tin. Bake for about 1¼ hours until just firm. Leave to cool in the tin.

2 Colour 350 g (12 oz) of the icing light brown, 225 g (8 oz) red, 100 g (3½ oz) light green, 50 g (2 oz) pale pink, 25 g (1 oz) dark green and 25 g (1 oz) yellow, leaving the rest white.

3 On a piece of greaseproof paper, draw around the end of the loaf tin. Extend the sides by

2.5 cm (1 inch) then join in a curve to make the headboard template. Roll out a little brown icing and cut a headboard. Leave to harden for 2-3 days.

4 Dampen the cake board. Roll out two-thirds of the red icing and cover the board. Slice the domed top off the cake; cut horizontally into three. Sandwich with half the butter cream and some jam. Spread the remaining butter cream over the top and sides. Roll out the remaining brown icing and cover the sides and one end of the cake. Place the cake on the cake board.

5 Roll out a red 'bottom sheet' 14 × 6 cm (5½ × 2½ inches). Reserve the trimmings. Dampen the top end of the cake and secure the sheet in place. Shape a pillow in white icing and secure square on the red sheet. Shape a ball of the pale pink icing and place on the pillow. Make a body shape in pink icing and place on the cake.

6 Roll out the light green icing to a 17 cm (6½ inch) square for the blanket. Roll out tiny balls of white and dark green icing and roll into the light green icing. Trim the edges. Drape the blanket over the bed. Roll out a strip of dark green icing, for the top edge.

7 Roll out the yellow icing into a rope then plait. Secure to the doll's head. Make a fringe, closed eyes, nose and mouth.

8 Dampen the top end of the cake. Press the headboard into position. Add two balls of red icing at each end of the headboard. Shape and secure red ribbons on to the plaits. Paint rosy cheeks.

HINT

Although this cake is easy to assemble, you'll need to make the headboard several days in advance to give it time to set hard.

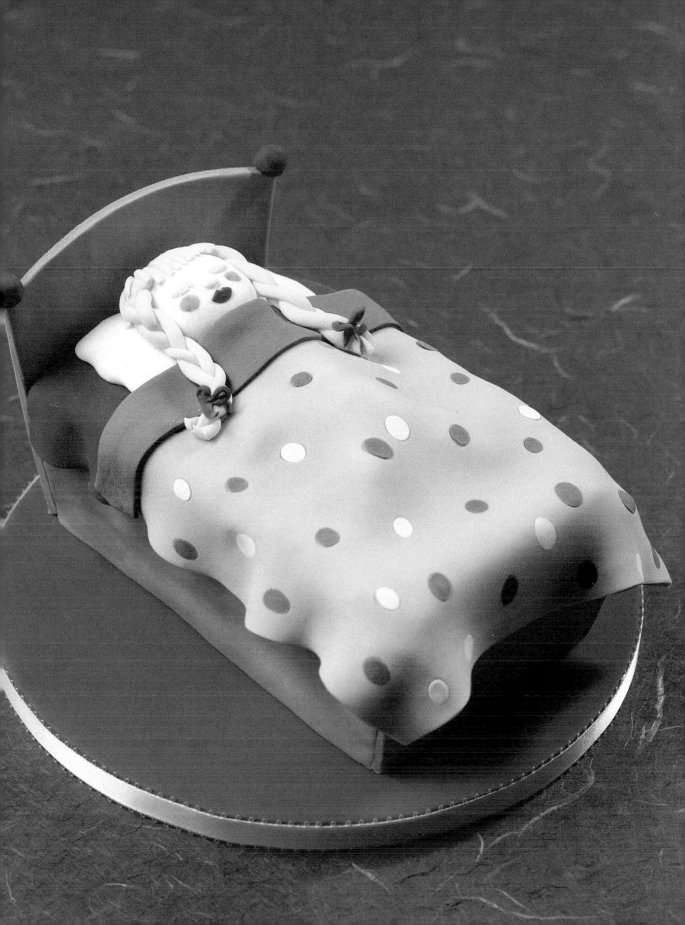

BEDTIME BEAR

This is a delicately coloured cake, ideal for a first birthday. You might like to colour it pale pink for a baby girl.

Madeira cake mixture made with 175 g (6 oz) plain flour (see pages 14–15)

1 quantity butter cream (see page 16)

jam, for filling

25 cm (10 inch) round cake board

1.25 kg (2 lb 12 oz) ready-to-roll icing

blue, brown and yellow food colourings

---

1 Make the cake mixture and turn into a prepared 20.5 cm (8 inch) round cake tin. Bake for about 1 1/2 hours or until the cake springs back when pressed gently in the centre. Leave to cool in the tin.

2 Slice the dome off the top of the cake. Halve the cake horizontally and sandwich with half the butter cream and the jam. Place on the cake board and spread with the remaining butter cream.

3 Colour 300 g (11 oz) of the icing blue, 100 g (3 1/2 oz) brown and 75 g (3 oz) yellow, leaving the remainder white.

4 Roll out the white icing and use to cover the cake, smoothing it to fit around the sides. Trim off the excess icing around the base and reserve. Leave to set overnight.

5 Roll out the blue icing to a 28 cm (11 inch) round. Lightly dampen the top of the cake and position the blue icing over it so the excess falls down the sides. Smooth the icing around the sides of the cake then, using the tip of a sharp knife, cut away scallops of icing, leaving neat points at different heights around the sides. Lightly dampen the cake board. Reroll the blue icing trimmings and use to cover the cake board, trimming off the excess around the edges.

6 Shape the teddy's head and body in brown icing, then two legs and ears and secure together. Sit the teddy on top of the cake.

7 Using the template on page 92, roll out yellow icing very thinly to a curved strip about 4 cm (1 1/2 inches) wide, 16 cm (6 1/2 inches) along the outer curve and 8 cm (3 1/4 inches) along the inner edge. Wrap around the teddy so it just overlaps at the front. Fold back the edges to make a collar. Roll out a little yellow icing, shape into a night cap and secure in position.

Roll a sausage of yellow icing, about 5 cm (2 inches) long and halve diagonally in the centre. Bend each piece and secure to teddy for arms. Flatten a small ball of white icing into a snout and position on the face. Secure another ball to the end of the night cap. Add two small balls of brown icing for paws.

8 Roll more balls of yellow icing and secure around the cake at the tips of the scallops. From the icing trimmings shape and position a small mug, book and blanket. Use food colouring to paint the teddy's features and buttons on the front of the night-shirt.

SEA SCENE

This is a cake that you can get really carried away with, adding fish, plants and shells in any colours and shapes that you wish.

Victoria sandwich cake mixture made with 225 g (8 oz) flour (see page 14)

1 quantity butter cream (see page 16)

jam, for filling

30 cm (12 inch) round cake board

1.3 kg (3 lb) ready-to-roll icing

blue, orange, green, yellow and red food colourings

small white or coloured candles

1 Make the cake mixture and turn into two prepared 20.5 cm (8 inch) round sandwich tins. Bake for about 30 minutes or until just firm to the touch. Turn out, remove the lining paper and leave to cool on a wire rack.

2 Sandwich the cakes with half the butter cream and the jam and place on the cake board. Spread with the remaining butter cream.

3 Colour 1 kg (2 lb 4 oz) of the ready-to-roll icing blue, 125 g (4 oz) orange, 50 g (2 oz) green, 50 g (2 oz) yellow and 50 g (2 oz) red. Leave a tiny amount white for the eyes of the octopus and fish and for the water ripples on the top of the cake.

4 Reserve 175 g (6 oz) of the blue icing. Roll out the remainder and use to cover the cake, smoothing it to fit around the sides. Trim off the excess icing around the base. Dampen the edges of the cake board. Roll out the remaining blue icing thinly and use to cover the edges of the board. Trim off the excess.

5 Roll about half the orange icing into a ball and make it slightly pear shaped at one end. Cut off an angled slice from the thin end and secure to the top of the cake. Roll the remaining orange icing into eight long tentacles, thinning each to a point at one end. Position each tentacle on the cake, wrapping the appropriate number of candles at the ends.

6 Roll out the green icing thinly and cut out seaweed shapes. Secure at various intervals around the sides of the cake.

7 From the remaining colours, shape a selection of different fish and starfish and secure around the sides. Add eyes to the octopus and fish and ripples on the surface of the cake in white icing. Use a fine paintbrush and diluted food colourings to paint the features on to the octopus' face.

HINT

As the octopus on this cake can hold a candle in each tentacle, it's ideal for any child up to the age of eight.

FRIENDLY TIGER

The tiger mouth candle holders create the perfect finishing touch for this stunning tiger's face cake.

Victoria sandwich cake mixture made with 125 g (4 oz) flour (see page 14)

15 g (¹/₂ oz) cocoa powder, sifted

chocolate and hazelnut spread, for filling

225 g (8 oz) ready-to-roll icing

yellow, black and pink food colourings

2 green jelly diamonds

2 pieces of uncooked white spaghetti

FROSTING

1 egg white

225 g (8 oz) caster sugar

a pinch of salt

a pinch of cream of tartar

30 ml (2 tbsp) water

---

1 Make the cake mixture and divide in half. Fold the cocoa powder into one half. Drop spoonfuls of the white cake mixture into a prepared 18 cm (7 inch) round cake tin. Drop spoonfuls of chocolate mixture to fill the gaps. Smooth the top of the cake. Bake at 190°C (375°F) Mark 5 for about 40 minutes or until well risen and firm to the touch. Cool on a wire rack.

2 Slice the cake in half horizontally and sandwich with the chocolate and hazelnut spread. Set on a cake board or a serving plate.

3 To make the frosting, put all the ingredients in a bowl and whisk lightly. Place over a pan of hot water and heat, whisking, until the mixture stands in peaks, about 7 minutes. Colour the frosting yellow and pour over the cake. Using a palette knife, spread the frosting to cover the cake, leaving it slightly 'fluffed up'.

4 Colour 75 g (3 oz) of the icing black, 25 g (1 oz) pink and 25 g (1 oz) yellow, and leave the rest white. Roll out the pink, yellow and a third of the white icing. Cut three 2 cm (³/₄ inch) pink rounds, two 5 cm (2 inch) yellow rounds and two 2.5 cm (1 inch) white. Gently pull the yellow rounds to a point at one end. Dampen in the centre and attach two pink circles. Pinch together at the bottom. Leave to dry over a rolling pin, pink side down, for about 30 minutes.

5 Put the white circles in place as eyes. Dampen and attach the jelly diamonds. Place the last pink circle as a tongue. Roll the remaining white icing into two

flattish balls for the tiger's cheeks. Mark with a skewer. Break the spaghetti into 10 cm (4 inch) lengths and insert as 'whiskers' into the sides of the cheeks.

6 Roll a little black icing into a nose, mark nostrils and position. Roll out the remaining black icing. Using a small and large round, fluted pastry cutter, cut out stripes as shown. Arrange them on the work surface to make sure they form a nice tiger pattern, then put in place on the cake.

7 To make the tiger mouth candle holders, use the trimmings from the pink and white icing. For each candle, make two pea-sized balls of white icing and cut one 5 mm (¹/₄ inch) round of pink. Dampen the side of the cake board or plate with a little water and press on the pink circles. Mark the white balls with a skewer and press them on top of the pink rounds. Secure the candles into the centre of the white balls.

SWEET CROWN

When you cut this stunningly decorated crown, the children can share out the sweets that nestle on the top.

Madeira cake mixture made with 175 g (6 oz) plain flour (see pages 14–15)

1 quantity butter cream (see page 16)

jam, for filling

25 cm (10 inch) round cake board

1.25 kg (2 lb 12 oz) ready-to-roll icing

purple, green and red food colourings

1/2 quantity royal icing (see page 16)

3 m (9 feet 10 inches) fine gold braid

a selection of brightly coloured boiled sweets and foil-wrapped chocolates

1 Make the cake mixture and turn into a prepared 20.5 cm (8 inch) round cake tin. Bake for 1 1/2 hours or until the cake springs back when pressed gently in the centre. Leave to cool in the tin.

2 Halve the cake horizontally and sandwich with half the butter cream and the jam. Place on the cake board and spread with the remaining butter cream. Colour 650 g (1 lb 7 oz) of the ready-to-roll icing green, 75 g (3 oz) red and the remainder purple.

3 Roll out the green icing and use to cover the cake, smoothing it to fit around the sides. Trim off the excess icing around the base.

4 Measure the circumference of the cake with string. Cut out greaseproof paper that length and 2.5 cm (1 inch) deeper than the cake. Roll out the purple icing and trim to the same size. Slide the paper under the icing strip. Using a sharp knife, cut a zigzag line along one edge, no deeper than 2.5 cm (1 inch) into the strip.

5 Dampen the sides of the cake. Lift the strip and secure it around the sides of the cake. (Get someone to help if necessary.) Leave the paper in place, sealing the ends together with sticky tape. Leave in a cool, dry place for 1–2 days until the icing is set, then remove the paper collar.

6 Dampen the edges of the cake board. Roll out the red icing and use to cover the edges.

7 Put the royal icing in a paper piping bag fitted with a writing nozzle. Unwrap some boiled sweets and secure around the sides of the cake at regular intervals using a little of the royal icing. Pipe some icing around one sweet and in a curvy line to the next sweet. Secure the gold braid around the sweet and over the piped line. Continue piping more lines and securing the braid all round the cake. Secure the remaining braid around the base of the cake, trimming the end to fit neatly. Pile sweets into the centre of the cake.

HINT

This cake can be decorated a week or two in advance, but leave the side decoration until only a couple of days before the party as boiled sweets soften once unwrapped.

DOG IN BED

This is an excellent choice for any child with a pet dog, especially if it is rather naughty.

Madeira cake mixture
made with 175 g (6 oz)
plain flour
(see pages 14–15)

1 quantity butter cream
(see page 16)

jam, for filling

850 g (1 lb 14 oz) ready-
to-roll icing

blue, cream, peach,
brown and black food
colourings

25 cm (10 inch) round
cake board

1 Prepare a 20.5 cm (8 inch) square cake tin even though the recipe is for an 18 cm (7 inch) tin. Make the cake mixture; turn into the tin. Bake for 1½ hours or until the cake springs back when pressed. Cool in the tin.

2 Cut 5 cm (2 inches) off one side so the cake is rectangular. Cut off the dome. Halve the cake horizontally; sandwich with half the butter cream and the jam.

3 Colour 275 g (9 oz) of the ready-to-roll icing light blue, 250 g (9 oz) peach, 150 g (5 oz) cream and 50 g (2 oz) brown.

4 Dampen the cake board. Roll out some blue icing and cut out a 20.5 cm (8 inch) round. Place on the board. Roll out a little of the cream icing and cut a long thin strip to cover the edges. Trim off the excess around the edges.

5 Place the cake on the cake board and spread with the remaining butter cream. Roll out the peach icing to a rectangle and lay over the cake so the icing falls in loose folds around the sides. Trim where necessary to fit, using a pair of scissors.

6 Shape a pillow in cream icing and position near one end of the cake. Using brown icing, make and position an oval shape for the body of the dog. Shape and position a head, ears and front legs. Mark the paws.

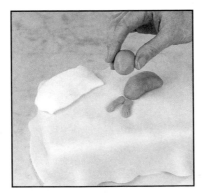

7 Roll out the blue icing to a 17 cm (6½ inch) square and drape over the bed so it comes slightly over the head of the dog. Roll out a long strip of cream icing and position along the top edge of the blanket.

8 Using black food colouring and a fine paintbrush, paint the features on the dog and paw marks over the bed and base.

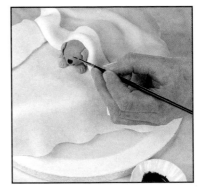

HINT

When making this cake, keep the colours to soft pastel shades, as in the photograph, or make them bright and bold.

HAUNTED CASTLE

This is a creepy cake to let your imagination run wild!
Definitely not for the faint-hearted!

Victoria sandwich cake mixture made with 275 g (10 oz) flour (see pages 14)

jam or chocolate spread, for filling

900 g (2 lb) ready-to-roll icing

purple, black and green food colourings

30 ml (2 tbsp) clear honey

12 red jelly diamonds

silver glitter dust

black candles

1 Grease and base line a 30.5 × 25 cm (12 × 10 inch) roasting tin and a 150 g (5 oz) food can. Make the cake mixture then half fill the food can and turn the rest into the roasting tin. Bake in the oven at 190°C (375°F) Mark 5 for about 20 minutes for the food can and for 45-60 minutes for the large cake. Cool on a wire rack.

2 Cut the large cake in half widthways and set on a cake board or serving plate. Spread with jam or chocolate spread. Break or cut the remaining sponge into pieces and pile on top of the base, securing with filling as you go. The result should be a lumpy mound of cake. Fix the small cake on top as a tower. Make a semicircular hollow at the front as a gateway.

3 Colour 50g (2 oz) of the ready-to-roll icing purple, 25 g (1 oz) black and the rest grey. Roll out the grey icing thinly. Add 15 ml (1 tbsp) water to the honey and heat until boiling. Brush the honey all over the cake and drape the rolled-out icing over, pressing it into the hollow at the front. Trim the icing at the base of the cake.

4 Roll out the purple icing and cut out to fill the hollow 'mouth'. Attach with the honey. Press the jelly diamonds into the edge of the mouth. Using diluted green food colouring, paint streaks of green 'slime'. Dust with the silver glitter.

5 With the icing trimmings, make spiders and snakes to crawl over the castle. Roll balls for candle holders and secure on top of the tower with hot honey.

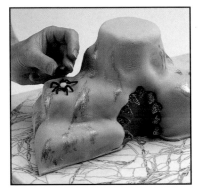

HINT
Add as many spiders and snakes as you like to this cake. Children will love them.

SHOOTING STARS

This cake is very simple, yet so effective as the deep blue colour of the background really sets off the white and silver stars.

Madeira cake mixture made with 175 g (6 oz) plain flour (see pags 14–15)

1 quantity butter cream (see page 16)

jam, for filling

33 cm (13 inch) round cake board

1 kg (2 lb 4 oz) ready-to-roll icing

dark blue, red, orange, black and silver food colourings

blue and silver floating candles or night-lights

1 Grease and base line a 3.4 litre (6 pint) ovenproof bowl. Make the cake mixture and turn into the bowl, levelling the surface. Bake for about 1½ hours until just firm. Leave to cool in the bowl, then loosen the edges with a palette knife to ease the cake out of the bowl.

2 Slice the dome off the top of the cake so that it sits flat, then cut the cake horizontally into three layers. Sandwich the layers together with half the butter cream and the jam and place on the cake board. Spread with the remaining butter cream.

3 Colour 900 g (2 lb) of the ready-to-roll icing dark blue, a small ball orange and a small ball red, leaving the remainder white.

4 Use a little of the blue icing to fill in any gaps left between the base of the cake and the board. Reserve 225 g (8 oz) of the icing and roll out the remainder. Use to cover the cake. Dampen the edges of the cake board. Roll out the remaining blue icing and use to cover the edges of the board, trimming off the excess.

5 From the white icing, shape a simple rocket and arrange at an angle on the cake. Shape several round stars and planets in the orange and red icing and secure. Roll some of the red and orange trimmings together to get a marbled effect on one of your planets. Roll out the white icing thinly and cut out a selection of small and large stars. Secure to the cake.

6 Using a fine paintbrush and silver food colouring, paint clusters of smaller stars on to the blue icing. Paint the details on the rocket. Arrange the candles around the cake board.

SNAKE IN THE GRASS

The colourful snake is set off beautifully against the green
'grass' base of this cake.

1 Make the cake mixture; turn
into two prepared 18 cm (7 inch)
round sandwich tins. Bake for
about 30 minutes until just firm to
the touch. Cool on a wire rack.

2 Sandwich the cakes with a little
of the butter cream and some
jam and place on the cake board.
Colour 150 g (5 oz) of the icing
light green, 150 g (5 oz) dark
green, 500 g (1 lb 2 oz) yellow,
50 g (2 oz) red and 25 g (1 oz)
black, leaving the remainder white.
Colour the remaining butter
cream green.

3 Using a palette knife, spread
the green butter cream all over
the top and sides of the cake in
an even layer. Spread a thin layer
on to the board. Lightly swirl the
butter cream all over with the tip
of the knife.

4 Press the wooden skewer into
the cake, about 2.5 cm (1 inch)
away from the edge. For the
snake, roll the yellow icing into a
ball, then roll under the palms of
your hands into a long thin
sausage about 50 cm (20 inches)
long, slightly thicker at one end
and tapering to a point at the
other. Arrange the snake in a coil
on the cake, first letting the thin
end meet the edge of the cake.
Then coil the snake around the
top of the cake and secure the
upright head end on to the
skewer. Using the tip of a knife,
cut a small smiling mouth.

5 Roll out the red icing thinly and
cut out a selection of triangles in
various sizes. Dampen the
underside of the triangles and
secure along the snake. Shape a
rectangle of red icing and secure
under the head. Position two
small balls of white icing for the
eyes.

6 Roll a long thin strip of black
icing and secure along the back of
the snake between the red
triangles. Using food colouring and
a fine paintbrush, paint the eyes.

7 Roll out the green icings thinly
and cut out long thin strips,
tapering to a point at one end.
Secure the strips around the sides
of the cake, pressing them slightly
into the butter cream to secure.
Mix the colours of the grass as
you work around the cake and let
some of them curl round on to
the cake board.

HINT

If you like, press some candles
into the cake board using a little
extra icing to make sure they are
secure.

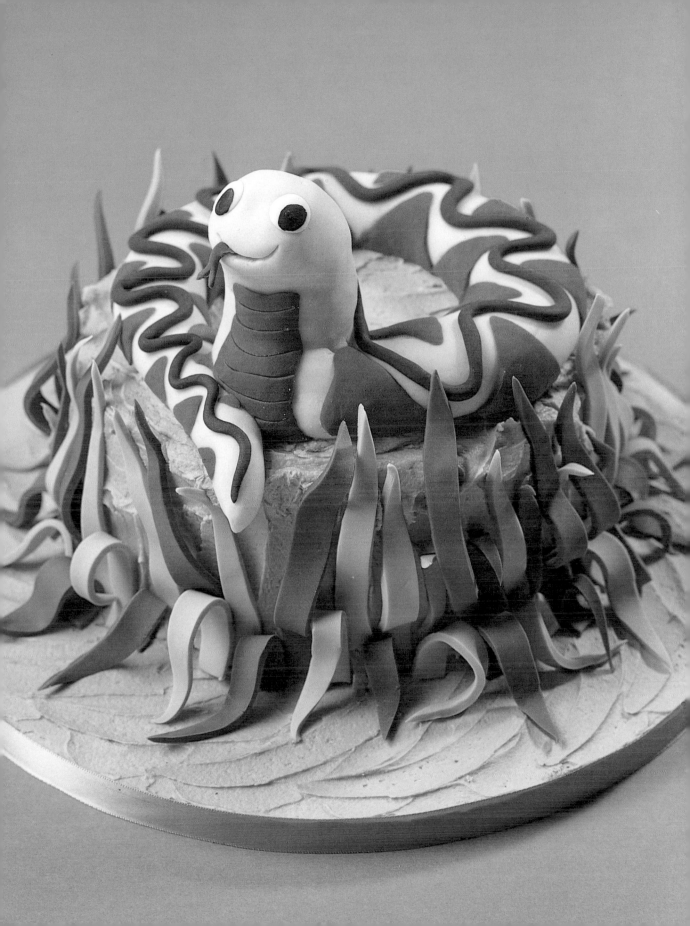

GOLD MEDAL

You can easily adapt the words on this 'World's Naughtiest Child' medal, to 'Greatest', 'Noisiest', or 'Best'!

> **Madeira cake mixture made with 225 g (8 oz) plain flour (see pages 14–15)**
>
> **1 quantity butter cream (see page 16)**
>
> **jam, for filling**
>
> **25 cm (10 inch) square cake board**
>
> **1.25 kg (2 lb 12 oz) ready-to-roll icing**
>
> **green and gold food colourings**
>
> **striped ribbon for medal and sides of cake**
>
> **green or gold braided rope for base of cake**

1 Make the cake mixture and turn into a prepared 20.5 cm (8 inch) square cake tin. Bake for about 1³/₄ hours or until the cake springs back when pressed gently in the centre. Leave to cool in the tin then turn out, peel off the lining paper and place on a wire rack to cool completely.

2 Slice the dome off the top of the cake. Halve the cake horizontally and sandwich with half the butter cream and the jam. Reserve 30 ml (2 tbsp) of the butter cream. Place the cake on the board and spread with the remaining butter cream. Colour 100 g (3¹/₂ oz) of the ready-to-roll icing green.

3 Reserve 75 g (3 oz) of the white ready-to-roll icing. Roll out the remainder and use to cover the cake, smoothing it to fit around the sides. Trim off the excess icing around the base of the cake.

4 Dampen the surface of the cake board with water. Roll out the green icing thinly and use to cover the edges of the board, trimming off the excess around the edges. Secure the braided rope around the base of the cake.

5 Roll out the reserved white icing to 3 mm (¹/₈ inch) thickness and cut out a circle using a 10 cm (4 inch) cutter or small bowl as a guide. Mark little grooves around the sides, and a small hole, 5 mm (¹/₄ inch) away from the edge for the ribbon. Lift the icing on to the top of the cake. Gently press a 4 cm (1¹/₂ inch) cutter into the centre of the 'medal'.

6 Cut two 20.5 cm (8 inch) lengths of the striped ribbon. Tuck one under the medal, behind the hole. Tuck the other into the hole to look as though it has been threaded through. Secure more ribbon around the sides of the cake.

7 Using gold food colouring, paint the medal and leave it to dry. Put the reserved butter cream in a piping bag fitted with a writing nozzle and use to pipe your chosen message on to the medal.

HINT

Instead of a 'joke' message on the medal, this cake design could be used for a specific purpose; for example, if a child has passed an exam or won a prize.

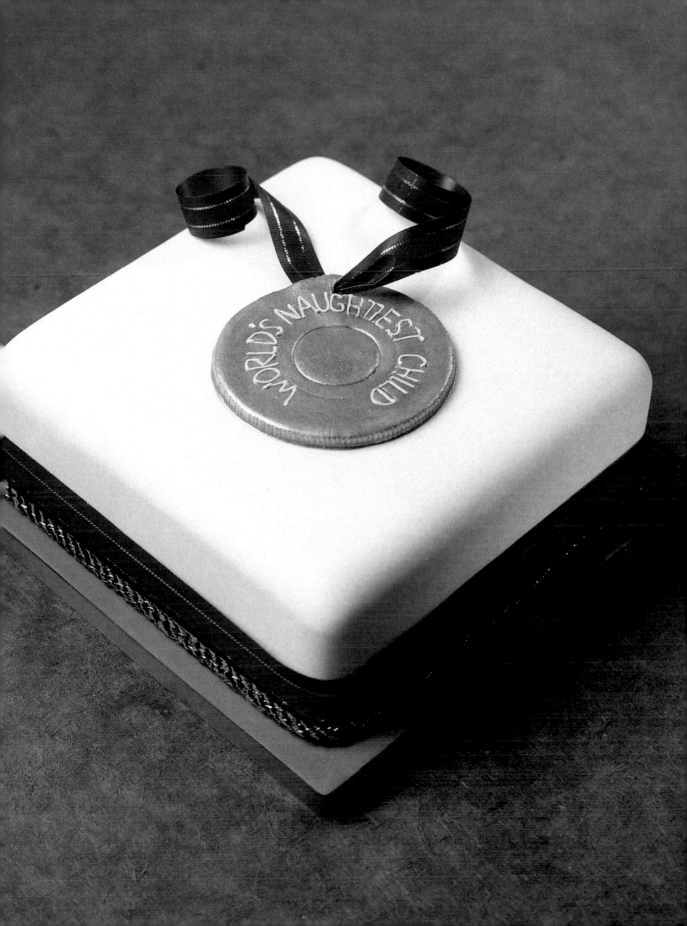

HOT WHEELS

This is a great cake idea for any child who's interested in fast cars. Use a different colour scheme if you prefer.

Madeira cake mixture made with 175 g (6 oz) plain flour (see pages 14–15)

1 quantity butter cream (see page 16)

jam, for filling

23 cm (9 inch) square cake board

1 kg (2 lb 4 oz) ready-to-roll icing

red, black, yellow, orange, yellow and silver food colourings

1 Make the cake mixture and turn into a prepared 18 cm (7 inch) square cake tin. Bake for 1½ hours until the cake springs back when pressed. Leave to cool in the tin then turn out.

2 Cut the dome off the top of the cake. Halve the cake horizontally and sandwich with some butter cream and jam. Then halve the cake vertically and sandwich the two layers together so the cake block is about 10 cm (4 inches) deep.

3 Cut out a wedge from one end of the cake for the bonnet area. Cut another wedge from under the bumper area at the front. Colour 450 g (1 lb) of the ready-to-roll icing red, 375 g (13 oz) black, 125 g (4 oz) grey (using a little black food colouring) and the remainder yellow.

4 Lightly dampen the cake board. Roll out the grey icing thinly and use to cover the board. Spread the remaining butter cream over the cake. Place on the board.

5 Roll out two-thirds of the red icing to a strip about 35 × 9 cm (14 × 3½ inches). Lay over the cake, starting at the bottom edge of the back, then laying it over the roof and front of the cake, tucking it under at the front. Trim off any excess. Use the remaining red icing to cover the sides of the cake. Leave for several hours to harden.

6 Roll out the yellow icing thinly. Dampen the front corners of the cake and lay the yellow icing over to cover the flame area. Using a scalpel or fine bladed knife, cut through the yellow icing to shape the flames, removing the excess icing. Shape more flames from the trimmings and secure on to the sides of the cake.

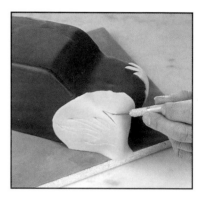

7 Thinly roll out some black icing and cut a long strip, about 2 cm (¾ inch) wide. Secure all around the base of the cake. Shape and position black icing for the windows.

8 Shape a long thin strip of black icing for the bumper and secure to the front of the cake. Divide the remaining black icing into four and shape each into large wheels. Make tyre markings with a knife and secure the wheels to the sides of the cake.

9 Using a fine paintbrush and silver food colouring, paint the window edges, bumper and wheel centres.

MUNCHER

This simple yet effective graphic design is taken from a popular computer game and is easily achieved. Use icing of any colour, the brighter the better!

Victoria sandwich cake mixture made with 350 g (12 oz) flour (see page 14)

jam, butter cream (see page 16) or chocolate spread, for filling

900 g (2 lb) ready-to-roll icing

bright green, yellow and black food colourings

30 ml (2 tbsp) clear honey

¼ quantity royal icing (see page 16)

---

1 Grease and base line a 25 cm (10 inch) and a 12.5 cm (5 inch) round cake tin. (If you do not have such a small tin, bake a slightly larger cake and cut it to size.) Make the cake mixture and divide between the two tins. The cakes should be quite shallow. Bake in the oven at 190°C (375°F) Mark 5, for 25 minutes for the small one and about 30 minutes for the larger one. Turn out, remove the lining paper and cool on a wire rack.

2 This cake needs a board about 28 × 51 cm (11 × 20 inches) or a serving plate. It may be a good idea to use a chopping board covered with foil. Slice both cakes in half horizontally and sandwich with your chosen filling. Cut a wedge (about one-eighth) from the large cake.

3 Reserve 25 g (1 oz) of the ready-to-roll icing and colour the rest the most fluorescent green possible. Divide into two pieces, one for the small and one for the large cake, and roll out into rounds. Add 15 ml (1 tbsp) water to the honey and heat until boiling. Brush over the cakes then cover with the icing.

4 As the larger cake has a wedge cut out, the icing will need to be cut and trimmed to fit. Trim the base edges. Lift the cakes on to the board or plate and arrange as though the large one is about to gobble up the smaller one.

5 Prepare a greaseproof paper piping bag fitted with a medium writing nozzle. Colour the royal icing a lively yellow. Pipe small bulbs of icing around the base and top edges of the cakes. On the small cake, pipe a wide open mouth too.

6 Colour a marble-sized piece of the reserved ready-to-roll icing black. Roll out the remaining icing and cut out two rounds. Position for an eye on each cake and attach with a little water. Roll out the black icing and cut small rounds for the pupils. Secure in position with water.

FOOTBALL MAD

This is a stunning cake for football fans,
boys and girls, of any age.

**Madeira cake mixture
made with 225 g (8 oz)
plain flour
(see pages 14–15)**

**1 quantity butter cream
(see page 16)**

jam, for filling

**30 cm (12 inch) round
cake board**

**1.5 kg (3 lb 6 oz) ready-
to-roll icing**

**black, green and red food
colourings**

---

1 Grease and base line a 3.4 litre (6 pint) ovenproof bowl. Make the cake mixture, turn into the bowl and level the surface. Bake for about 1½ hours or until just firm. Cool in the bowl.

2 Slice the dome off the top of the cake so that it sits flat on the surface, then cut the cake horizontally into three layers. Sandwich with half the butter cream and the jam and place on the cake board. Spread with the remaining butter cream. Colour 175 g (6 oz) of the ready-to-roll icing black, 150 g (5 oz) green and 75 g (3 oz) red, leaving the remainder white.

3 Roll out 450 g (1 lb) of the white icing thinly and use to cover the cake, smoothing the sides and trimming off the excess. (Don't worry about getting a perfect finish; the icing will be covered.)

4 Roll out half the black icing and half the remaining white icing. Cut out hexagon shapes using the template on page 92 as a guide. Lightly dampen the cake surface and secure the hexagons to the top of the cake, shaping the pattern so that each black hexagon is surrounded by white hexagons. Continue covering the cake with the shapes, using the remaining icing as you work down the sides. (The shapes become slightly more difficult to fit as you work around the sides, but ease them into place and trim where you need to.)

5 Roll out the green icing thinly and use to cover the edge of the cake board, trimming off the excess. If liked, use the green icing trimmings to shape 'grass' and secure around the ball.

6 For the rosette, roll out the red icing and cut out a long thin strip. Pleat it up slightly as you form it into a round and secure to the side of the football. Shape two ribbons and arrange them to one side, then position a circle of red icing in the centre.

HINT

Don't forget to check the child's favourite football team colours before you make the rosette, which could be in more than one colour if necessary.

FLOWERPOT

In this eye-catching cake, you can alter the colours to suit the child, depending on whether soft pastels or stronger shades are preferred. Bake the cake base in a new, thoroughly washed, terracotta flowerpot.

Madeira cake mixture made with 125 g (4 oz) plain flour (see pages 14–15)

½ quantity butter cream (see page 16)

jam, for filling

900 g (2 lb) ready-to-roll icing

red, brown, green, orange and pink food colourings

18 cm (7 inch) round cake board

Smarties

1 Grease and line the base and sides of a terracotta flowerpot, measuring 12 cm (4½ inches) deep and 13 cm (5 inches) across the top. Grease and base line a 600 ml (1 pint) ovenproof bowl. Make the cake mixture and turn it into the pot and bowl. Bake, allowing about 45 minutes for the bowl and 1 hour for the pot. Leave to cool in the containers.

2 Colour 500 g (1 lb 2 oz) of the ready-to-roll icing terracotta colour using about one part red colouring to two parts brown. Colour 200 g (7 oz) dark green, 75 g (3 oz) orange, 75 g (3 oz) pink, leaving the remainder white. Lightly dampen the cake board. Roll out some green icing and use to cover the board, trimming off the excess around the edges.

3 Slice the flowerpot cake horizontally into three and sandwich with half the butter cream and the jam. Spread a little more butter cream around the sides of the cake. Reserve 50 g (2 oz) of the terracotta icing and roll out the remainder to a long, slightly curved strip, about 11 cm (4½ inches) wide and about 35 cm (14 inches) long. Roll the cake in the strip, trimming off the excess where the ends meet. Reserve the trimmings. Transfer the cake to the board. Roll out the trimmings to a long strip, about 2.5 cm (2 inches) wide and the circumference of the top of the cake. Dampen the top edge of the cake with water and secure the strip in position.

4 Trim the smaller cake so it sits comfortably inside the rim of the base and spread with the remaining butter cream. Roll out the remaining green icing and use to cover the cake.

5 Roll out a little of the orange, pink and white icing and cut out flowers using a cutter, about 5 cm (2 inches) in diameter. Press gently on to the cake securing with a dampened paintbrush. Press a Smartie into the centre of each as you work. Roll out the remaining icing and use to cover the rest of the cake with flowers.

HINT

If you liked, you could tie a ribbon around the flowerpot just under the rim, and finish it in a bow.

DINOSAUR EGG

Ever popular with boys and girls, this prehistoric-look cake takes a
little time and trouble - but it is well worth the effort.

700g (1½ lb) ready-to-roll icing

purple, yellow, blue and black food colourings

Victoria sandwich cake mixture made with 175 g (6 oz) flour (see page 14)

½ quantity butter cream (see page 16)

30 ml (2 tbsp) clear honey

30.5 x 20.5 cm (12 x 8 inch) cake board (optional)

a little royal icing (see page 16)

1 Make the dinosaur at least three days in advance and leave to dry. Colour 125 g (4 oz) of the ready-to-roll icing purple. Roll one large sausage and a small one about the size of your little finger. Curl them round and pull spikes of icing up on the back. Make the small one pointed at one end for a tail. Cut a slit in one end of the large one for a mouth.

2 It is possible to hire egg-shaped cake moulds; otherwise use two 1.1 litre (2 pint) pudding basins. The mould only needs greasing; the basins should be greased and base lined. Make the cake mixture and divide between the tins or basins. Bake at 190°C (375°F) Mark 5 for 35-40 minutes. Turn out, remove the lining paper, if used, and cool on a wire rack.

3 Colour 125 g (4 oz) of the remaining ready-to-roll icing yellow and the rest turquoise (by mixing blue and yellow together). Only partly mix the colouring in so that the icing is marbled.

4 The finished egg will lie on its side. Slice off a small piece of cake from one side to prevent the egg wobbling about on the cake board or plate. Halve the cakes horizontally, then sandwich the pieces together with the butter cream.

5 Roll out the turquoise icing. Add 15 ml (1 tbsp) water to the honey and heat until boiling then brush over the egg. Lay the icing over the egg and smooth it to fit. You will need to trim off the excess icing, make a few pleats and smooth over the joins with a palette knife. Tuck the ends underneath the egg. With a sharp knife, cut a zigzag down the middle of the egg, as though it has been cracked open, and ease it apart. Remove one or two of the zigzag points to create a space for the dinosaur. Place on the cake board, if using, or a serving plate.

6 Use a little of the yellow icing to make a tongue for the dinosaur and secure inside the mouth. Using a cheese grater, grate the rest of the yellow icing. Pile some into the open crack to represent the inside of the egg, letting it spill over on to the board if liked. Position the dinosaur and the tail in the egg, rearranging the grated icing as necessary. Colour a little royal icing black. Pipe the eyes using white and black royal icing.

KEYBOARD

This is an impressive cake for slightly older children. Personalise it by adding the colours and shapes on the recipient's own keyboard.

1 Make the cake mixture and turn into a prepared 18 cm (7 inch) square cake tin. Bake for about 1½ hours or until the cake springs back when lightly pressed in the centre. Leave to cool in the tin, then remove from the tin.

2 Cut the dome off the top of the cake, then halve the cake horizontally. Place the two pieces side by side on the board, securing the ends together with butter cream. Cut a 26 x 9 cm (10½ x 3½ inch) rectangle out of the front side of the cake, about 1 cm (½ inch) deep. Spread the cake with the remaining butter cream. Colour 825 g (1 lb 13 oz) of the ready-to-roll icing black, 200 g (7 oz) blue, 50 g (2 oz) purple and a tiny piece red, leaving the remainder white.

3 Reserve 150 g (5 oz) of the black icing. Roll out the remainder and use to cover the top and sides of the cake, smoothing down the icing around the sides and trimming off the excess. Flatten and smooth the icing as much as possible and accentuate the edges as corners with your fingers.

4 Roll out the white icing to a 24 x 7 cm (9½ x 2¾ inch) rectangle, trimming the edges as neatly as possible. Lift into position over the cut-out area of the cake. Mark the white keys with a knife.

5 Roll more black icing to 5 mm (¼ inch) thick and then cut out 4.5 cm x 5 mm (1¾ x ¼ inch) pieces. Position over the white keys securing with water.

6 From the remaining black icing, cut out a 'speaker' panel and mark lines over it using the back of a knife. Position on the left-hand side of the cake. Position another black panel across the top of the cake, adding a smaller purple panel over this. Use more icing trimmings to add small controls.

7 Using a fine paintbrush and food colouring, paint words on the panel. Lightly dampen the board. Roll out the blue icing and use to cover the board, trimming off the excess around the edges.

HINT
To personalise the cake even more, write a message to the recipient on the white keys.

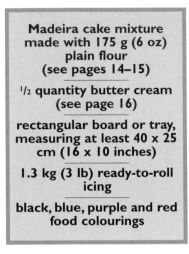

BIRTHDAY PRESENT

Older children might like this impressive-looking cake. Use a colour scheme and pattern to suit the child. The star shapes are made using icing dipped in coloured dusting powder (see page 12) to give a 'potato printed' effect.

**Madeira cake made with
250 g (9 oz) plain flour
(see pages 14–15)**

**1 quantity butter cream
(see page 16)**

jam, for filling

**28 cm (11 inch) square
cake board**

**1.25 kg (2 lb 12 oz)
ready-to-roll icing**

**blue and cream food
colourings**

orange dusting powder

30 ml (2 tbsp) icing sugar

**1 m (3 feet 2½ inches)
wide blue ribbon**

**1 m (3 feet 2½ inches) of
4 cm (1½ inch) wide blue
ribbon**

**1.5 m (4 feet 10¼ inches)
of 2.5 cm (1 inch) wide
orange ribbon, preferably
wired**

**silver ribbon for base of
cake**

1 Make the cake mixture and turn into a prepared 23 cm (9 inch) square cake tin. Bake for about 1¾ hours or until the cake springs back when pressed gently in the centre. Leave to cool in the tin then turn out, remove the lining paper and place on a wire rack to cool completely.

2 Halve the cake horizontally and sandwich with half the butter cream and the jam. Place on the cake board and spread with the remaining butter cream. Colour 1.1 kg (2 lb 6 oz) of the ready-to-roll icing blue and 125 g (4 oz) cream, leaving a small piece white.

3 Roll out the blue icing and use to cover the cake, smoothing it to fit around the sides. Trim off the excess icing around the base and leave to harden for several hours or overnight.

4 Dampen the edges of the cake board. Roll out the cream icing thinly and use to cover the board, trimming off the excess around the edges.

5 From the white icing press out two or three star shapes. Dip one in the dusting powder and gently press it on to the surface of the blue icing. Continue over the top and sides of the cake, using a new star shape when the first starts to loose its shape.

6 Blend the icing sugar with a little water to make a thin paste. Cut the wide ribbon to fit over the top and sides of the cake and secure at the base with a little icing paste. Secure the orange ribbon over the blue, adding a bow on top of the parcel. (If the ribbons don't stay in place around the sides, secure with some dressmakers' pins, then twist them out once the icing paste has set.) Secure the ribbon around the base of the cake.

HINT

If you can't get dusting powder for the star shapes, impress the cutter into the icing to leave an outline, then paint the shapes in gold or a darker shade of blue.

CD PLAYER

This really easy cake can be put together in an hour or two. For a personalised touch, write a message on the CDs.

Victoria sandwich cake mixture made with 225 g (8 oz) flour (see page 14)

1 quantity butter cream (see page 16)

30 cm (12 inch) square cake board

750 g (1 lb 10 oz) ready-to-roll icing

yellow, black, purple, silver and brown food colourings

1 liquorice Catherine wheel

1 Grease and line a 15 cm (6 inch) square cake tin and a 25 cm (10 inch) square tin or large roasting tin. Make the cake mixture and turn a 1 cm ($^1/_2$ inch) depth of mixture into the small tin, then the remainder into the large tin. Bake at 180°C (350°F) Mark 4 for 20-25 minutes until just firm. Leave to cool in the tins.

2 Using a knife, round off two of the corners on the small cake to make a CD player shape. Square off the sides of the larger cake if made in a roasting tin and put on the cake board. Spread with three-quarters of the butter cream. Colour 375 g (13 oz) of the ready-to-roll icing yellow, 250 g (9 oz) black and 125 g (4 oz) purple.

3 Roll out the yellow icing and use to cover the cake on the board, trimming off the excess around the base. Using a 10 cm (4 inch) cutter or small bowl as a guide, mark a CD outline on to the icing, then carefully mark a semicircle for a CD underneath it.

4 Spread the small cake with the remaining butter cream. Reserve 50 g (2 oz) of the black icing. Roll out the remainder and use to cover the cake, trimming off the excess around the base. Slide a fish slice under the cake and position on the yellow base.

5 Use the reserved black icing to shape the features of the player, starting with the lid, then the controls, securing with a dampened paintbrush. Lightly dampen the cake board. Roll out the purple icing and use to cover the board, trimming off the excess around the edges.

6 Use the silver, black and brown colourings to paint the discs and features on the player.

7 Unroll the liquorice and cut in half. Shape two small ear pieces in black icing trimmings and press a piece of liquorice into each. Tuck the ends of the liquorice into the back of the player.

WRESTLING RING

This is a cake to make by someone interested in moulding as the figures require a little time. It is a fun cake and will be a big hit with boys of all ages.

Victoria sandwich cake mixture made with 350 g (12 oz) flour (see page 14)

jam, chocolate spread or ½ quantity butter cream (see page 16), for filling

35 mm (12 inch) square cake board (optional)

900 g (2 lb) ready-to-roll icing

blue, yellow and purple food colourings

125 g (4 oz) marzipan (see page 17)

30 ml (2 tbsp) clear honey

4 satay sticks

8 drinking straws

2 wrestling figures (see page 19)

1 Make the cake mixture and turn into the prepared 23 cm (9 inch) square cake tin. Bake for about 1 hour, covering the top of the cake if it browns too quickly. Turn out, remove the lining paper and cool on a wire rack.

2 Slice the cake in half and sandwich with the filling. Place on the cake board, if using, or a plate. Colour 800 g (1¾ lb) of the ready-to-roll icing sky blue and 125 g (4 oz) bright yellow. Colour the marzipan purple.

3 Add 15 ml (1 tbsp) water to the honey and heat until boiling. Brush over the top and sides of the cake. Roll out the blue icing and cover the cake, smoothing the tops and sides. Cut and trim the corners to fit, then smooth the joins with a palette knife.

4 Using a ruler, mark the centre of the cake. Cut a large star out of the centre of the blue icing with a cutter or with a knife using a star-shaped cardboard template. Roll out the yellow icing. Using the same cutter or template, cut out a yellow star and place in the cut-out space, smoothing to fit.

5 With the remaining yellow icing, cut out lots of stars with a small cutter. Brush a very small amount of honey around the base of the cake and secure the stars.

6 Put a satay stick into each corner of sponge, pushing them right down to the bottom. Trim the tops so that they stand about 7.5 cm (3 inches) above the cake. Divide the marzipan into four. Roll into sausages and fit over the exposed sticks. Trim the straws so that they are just a little longer than the gaps between the marzipan buffers. Carefully press them well into the marzipan with two on each side. Position the wrestling figures on top.

HINT
Remove the satay sticks from the cake before cutting and serving.

RUGBY PLAYER

The more mud splattered this cake, the more effective it'll be! Change the hair and rugby kit colourings to suit the recipient.

Madeira cake mixture made with 175 g (6 oz) plain flour (see pages 14–15)

1 quantity butter cream (see page 16)

jam, for filling

28 cm (11 inch) square cake board

1 kg (2 lb 4 oz) ready-to-roll icing

green, brown, flesh coloured (if available), black and blue food colourings

1 Make the cake mixture, turn into a prepared 25 cm (10 inch) square cake tin and bake for about 1½ hours or until the cake springs back when pressed. Cool in the tin. Cut a third off the cake. Halve both pieces horizontally. Place one large piece of cake on the board and spread with a little butter cream and jam. Place the two smaller pieces on top, side by side, spread with more filling and cover with the remaining cake. Spread with the remaining butter cream.

2 Colour 700 g (1 lb 9 oz) of the icing green, 125 g (4 oz) dark brown, 100 g (3½ oz) flesh coloured (see Hint on page 36), 25 g (1 oz) black, 15 g (½ oz) light brown, leaving the remainder white. Roll out the green icing cover the cake and board, trimming off the excess.

3 Roll out about one-third of the dark brown icing to an oval shape of 15 × 11 cm (6 × 4½ inches). Cut around the edges in a wavy line then position on top of the cake, securing with a dampened paintbrush. Shape small 'teardrop' shapes in brown icing and secure around the brown icing patch. Use the remaining brown icing to shape and position more muddy areas around the sides of the cake.

4 Shape a small round head, about 2 cm (¾ inch) in diameter and position on the cake. Add the top half of the body, measuring 4.5 × 4 cm (1¾ × 1½ inches) cutting it off at the waist. Shape a pair of shorts using 40 g (1½ oz) white icing.

5 Shape and secure two legs, bending one at the knee and propping it up on a ball of crumpled cling film so that it sets in position.

6 Shape a rugby ball in light brown icing and secure about 1 cm (½ inch) away from the top of the head. Shape two bent arms in white icing and secure to the body. Shape socks and press on to the ends of the legs. Roll more white icing and cut out the shirt, using the template on page 92 as a guide. Secure around the body.

7 Shape the hands and boots and secure in position. Shape the hair and secure on the head, with a thin strip of white for the headband. Using a paintbrush and brown food colouring, paint plenty of 'mud' on to the player.

TEMPLATES

RUGBY PLAYER
(page 90)

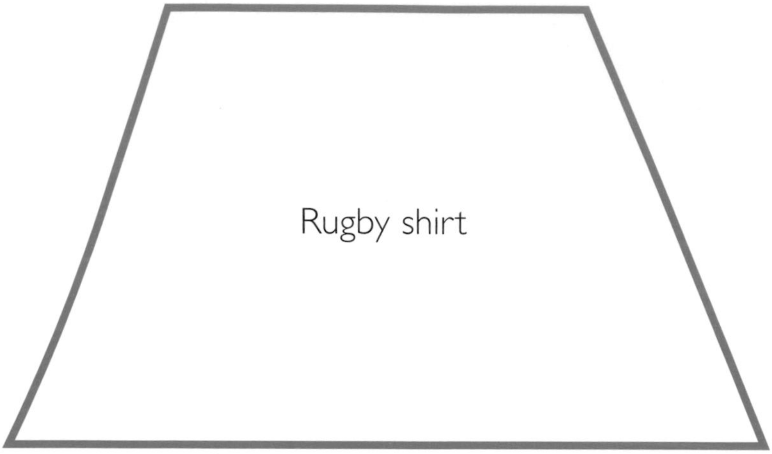

Rugby shirt

BEDTME BEAR
(page 54)

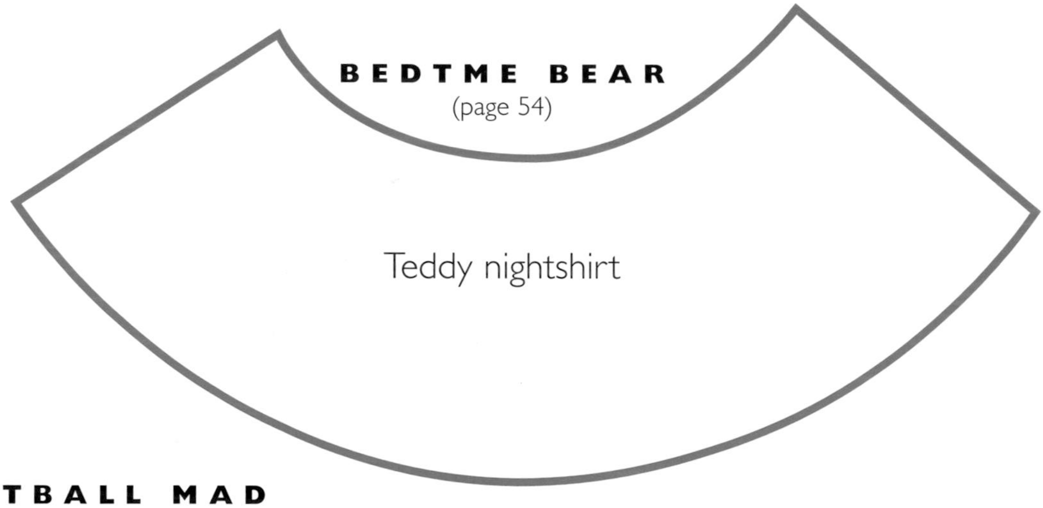

Teddy nightshirt

FOOTBALL MAD
(page 76)

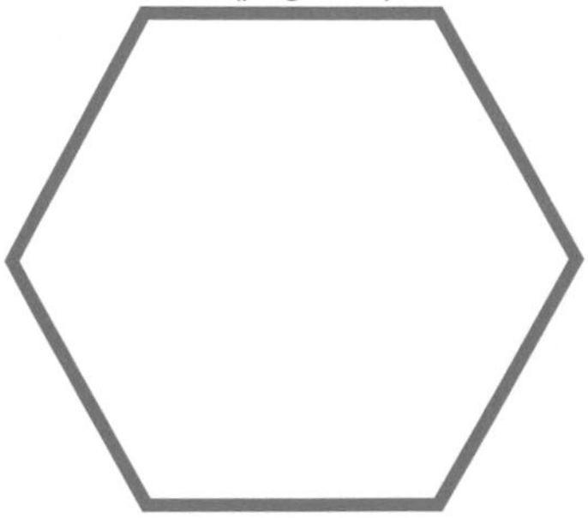

HAPPY HOUSE
(page 26)

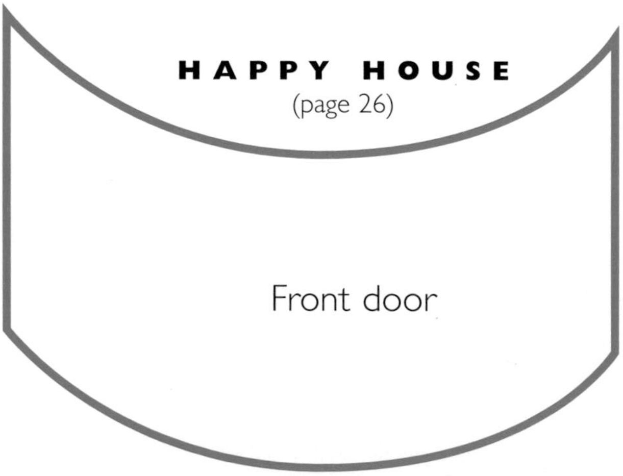

Front door

INDEX

SUPPLIERS AND USEFUL ADDRESSES

Bromley Cake Craft
7 Chatterton Road
Bromley
Kent
BR2 9QW
Tel: 0181 313 0090

The Cake Artistry Centre Ltd
906 Christchurch Road
Pokesdown
Bournemouth
Dorset
BH7 6DL
Tel: 01202 418370

G T Culpitt & Son Ltd
Culpitt House
Place Farm
Wheathamstead
Hertfordshire
AL4 8SB
Tel: 01582 834122

Squires Kitchen
Squires House
3 Waverley Lane
Farnham
Surrey
GU9 8BB
Tel: 01252 734309
Mail order service available.